# ENTREPRENEURSHIP AND ECONOMIC DEVELOPMENT

# Entrepreneurship and Economic Development

*Edited by :*

J. V. PRABHAKARA RAO

KANISHKA PUBLISHERS, DISTRIBUTORS
NEW DELHI-110 002

**KANISHKA PUBLISHERS, DISTRIBUTORS**
4697/5-21 A, Ansari Road, Daryaganj
New Delhi-110 002
Phones : 2327 0497, 2328 8285
Fax : 011-2328 8285
E-mail : kanishka_publishing@yahoo.co.in

First Published 2000
Second Edition 2008

ISBN 81-7391-332-3

PRINTED IN INDIA

Published by Madan Sachdeva for Kanishka Publishers, Distributors, 4697/5-21A, Ansari Road, Daryaganj, New Delhi-110 002, Typeset by Sunshine Graphics, Delhi, and Printed at Nice Printing Press, Delhi.

# Preface

Global business environment has been witnessing a sea change in terms of several aspects. In order to adapt to the rapidly changing environmental factors the business enterprises have been continuously striving towards better performance. Several countries across the globe have concentrated on building on their economic strength through the process of rapid economic growth to ensure their survival in the tumultuous international scenario. They have invariably accepted the fact that industrialisation is a pivotal factor for achieving the desired rate of economic growth and entrepreneurship is one of the most effective devices to foster/nurture industrial growth.

There are abundant examples to establish the fact that entrepreneurship has been the backbone of national development. Research studies conducted in this area have further established the fact that entrepreneurship can be cultivated, contrary to the earlier belief that entrepreneurs are a special creed and are born with these traits. Therefore, there is an ardent need to encourage entrepreneurship in our country also. This, however, is possible only when the right kind of climate, conducive for entrepreneurial growth, is created through favourable policy measures. There should be adequate provision of training and guidance facilities to individuals with entrepreneurial aptitude.

The present book is a collection of some of the papers presented during a 2-day National Seminar (sponsored by AICTE) on 31st August-1st September '98. The seminar aimed at creating an awareness about the need for entrepreneurial development in a developing country like India and its impact on the economic development of a nation. The papers are a reflection of the problems associated with entrepreneurship in India.

The book therefore presents a very authentic, data based, first hand analysis of the pace of entrepreneurial development in India while comparing it with other countries and analysing its impact on the country. The articles have been slightly edited to suit the objectives of the book.

I wish to express my appreciation to the All India Council for Technical Education for the financial support extended by them for conducting the seminar. I am grateful to Prof. R. Radha Krishna, Vice-Chancellor, Andhra University who has offered extensive help in this endeavour. I also take this opportunity to thank Prof. V. Balamohan Das, Dean, Faculty of Commerce and Management Studies and Prof. G. Subrahmanyam, Principal, Arts College, Andhra University, who have been a constant inspiration behind the conduct of the seminar. I thank Prof. K.C. Reddy, Director, School of Economics, who has given valuable suggestions at appropriate times.

**EDITOR**

# Contents

# List of Contributors

1. Dr. A.K. Choudhary, Faculty, Dept. of Commerce & Business Management, Vinoba Bhave University, Hazaribagh, (Bihar)
2. Prof. B. Ramachandra Reddy, S. K. Institute of Management, S. K. University, Anantapur, (A. P.)
3. D. Selvanayakam, Lecturer in Commerce, Loyola College, Chennai and Research Scholar, Chennai, (T. N.)
4. Dr. G. P. Prasain, Asst. Professor, Dept. of Commerce, Manipur University Imphal, (Manipur)
5. Dr. I. Parthasarathi, Principal, Dr. L.B. College, Visakhapatnam, (A. P.)
6. Prof. J.V. Prabhakara Rao, Head of the Department, Dept. of Commerce and Mgt. Studies, Andhra University, Visakhapatnam, (A. P.)
7. Dr. Khursheed A. Bhat, Reader, Dept. of Commerce, Kashmir University, Sringar, (J & K)
8. Prof. K. Seshaiah, Dept. of Commerce, S. V. University, Tirupati, (A. P.)
9. K. Srinivasa Rao, Manager (Finance), Hindustan Aeronautics Ltd., Bangalore, (Karnataka)
10. Prof. L. Venugopal Reddy, S.K. Institute of Management, S.K. University, Anantapur, (A. P.)
11. Dr. M. Munirami Reddy, Dept. of Commerce, S. V. University, Tirupati, (A. P.)
12. Dr. M. Panduranga Vithal, Professor of Finance and Strategy, Indian Institute of Plantation Management, Bangalore, (Karnataka)
13. Prof. N.C. Das, Ex. Dean, Faculty of Commerce, Guwahati University, Guwahati, (Assam)
14. Dr. N.P. Srinivasan, Professor & Head Dept. of Commerce, University of Madras, (T. N.)

15. Dr. P. Palanichamy, Reader in Commerce, Pondicherry University, Pondicherry.
16. Prof. P. Seshanjaneyulu, M.D., Yesses Annodizing Industry, Anantapur, (A. P.)
17. Dr. P.S. Tripathi, Faculty Member, FMS, Banaras Hindu University, Varanasi, (U. P.)
18. Mr. R. Duraipandian, (Junior Research Fellow), Alagappa Institute of Management, Alagappa University, (T. N.)
19. Dr. R.K. Pandey, Faculty of Management Studies, Banaras Hindu University, Varanasi, (U. P.)
20. Dr. R. Sreenivasagalu, Research Scholar, Lectureer in Commerce, Presidency College, Chennai, (T. N.)
21. Dr. R. Satya Raju, Professor, Dept. of Commerce & Mgt. Studies, Andhra University, Visakhapatnam, (A. P.)
22. Mrs. R. Vijaya, Head, MBA Programme, Samatha P.G. College , Visakhapatnam, (A. P.)
23. Dr. S. Arumugam, Prespective, Senior Project Leader & Head, Entrepreneurship Development Cell, Anna University, Chennai, (T. N.)
24. Dr. S.C. Sharma, Faculty, Markhem College of Commerce, Vinoba Bhave University, Hazaribagh, (Bihar)
25. Dr. S. Ganesan, (Reader & Director 1/c), Alagappa Institute of Management, Alagappa University, (T. N.)
26. Dr. S. Moharana, Professor and Co-ordinator, Dept. of Commerce, Utkal University, Bhubaneswar, (Orrisa)
27. Dr. S. Rajani, Lecturer, Pydah P.G. College, (Affiliated to Andhra University), Visakhapatnam, (A. P.)
28. V. Balakrishnan, Reader in Business Administration, Annamalai University, (T. N.)
29. Dr. V. G. Patel, Director, Entrepreneurship Development, Institute of India, Ahmedabad, (Gujrat)
30. Dr. V.K. Bhaskara Rao, Reader, P.G. Dept. of Commerce, VRS and YRN College Chirala, (T. N.)
31. V. Lakshmana Rao, Department of Economices, Andhra University, (A. P.)
32. V. Surya Rao, Manager (Finance), Housing Urban Development Corporation, New Delhi

# 1

# Introduction

*—V.G. Patel*

1. Withdrawal of special concessions and protection to small enterprises (from Internal Competition) and market protection to the large enterprises (from Global competition), combined with new rules of International Trade (GATT and WTO), technological pressures (Trips), and financial inflows (Trims) will shake Indian Entrepreneurship from its foundation. The process has already begun with number of small, medium and large businesses closing down, merging or giving up the fight by sell off.
2. Entrepreneurial movement and profiles will take different direction and shape in the coming decades. Traditional trade to manufacturing movement will be thwarted as capital owners with commercial knowledge give way to technocrats and professionals with insight into technology and management, educated and Techno-managerially qualified will prevail in the small and medium sector while artisans, craftsmen and low educated merchants and technicians may be pushed to tiny and micro enterprises education, unlike in the past, will acquire new significance as ability to locate, absorb and analyze information and respond to change, will determine business success and growth.
3. Family business, dominating Indian Business Scenario till now (95 per cent of total) will come under severe threat with disappearance of oligopolistic markets. The new competitive scenario would bring out (as it already has) inadequacies of

traditional business knowledge, styles and structures. New products, new technology, new capital sources and new markets would call for new knowledge, new personnel and different management practices. The automatic transition of business ownership (in family business) would expose how unprepared (ungroomed) the new generation has been to perform in the environment.

4. These entrepreneurs will have to survive two growth crises in the next few years : *(i)* prosperity crisis, and *(ii)* leadership crisis. A number of successful business enterprises may fail because of 'Complacency' or 'Sluggishness' arising out of regular and assured profits, resulting from large market shares, established brand names and life styles of rich and famous; or 'Cockiness' (Over-confidence) based on past successes leading to overambitious expansions, diversification into unrelated lines, and growth by leaps and bounds.
5. On the other hand, 'leadership crisis originating from failure to delegate and develop teams of managers and executives to plan and manage growth will be one of the critical personal as well as organisational challenges Indian Entrepreneurs will face.

   Studies show that from "owner-manager" to "owner-leader" is a transition only 30 per cent successfully make on their own. They survive and grow while another 30 per cent can be saved by sound advice and counselling. They are willing to change old styles, acquire new knowledge and retrain and discipline themselves. But a large 40 per cent cannot shed old habits and practices. These must not grow or they may perish.
6. What will critically distinguish 'high performers' from 'poor performers' in the future? Would it be better knowledge and information ? Better managerial and technical skills ? These two may not be adequate in the rapidly changing global environment. "Soft skill competencies" (Combining knowledge, skill and motivation/Attitude) will determine success and higher achievements. Proponents of competency based strategic management refer to recognising change in internal (firm level) and external (Industrial level) environment of business. An international study in three continents and three cultures including India has identified 13 soft skills competencies, possession of which have distinguished

higher performers from low performers in business.

7. Importance of soft-skill competencies would also mean a new profile of a desirable business manager. The manager in demand (MBAs) will not be the one who possesses the same knowledge and skill like 10,000 others, but the one who has the right kind of attitude, creativity, initiative, commitment and adaptability. Companies will not be satisfied with the intelligent, but high flying, inflexible, arrogant business graduates lacking in soft skills and jumping from Job to Job. In short, 'Intrapreneurs' will be in demand rather than pure managers.
8. On the technology front a serious threat is expected from the new rules of International trade and the patent regime as markets become global; capital products and technology flow from West to East and North to South and 'Process' gives way to 'products' patents restricting opportunities. Size of enterprise will change, large will become larger; small may become tiny, serving local markets and low cost need. Indian Entrepreneurs have not experienced the kind of huge investments, marketing resources and management practices, which go with them. They have three options :

   *(i)* Unprepared and overwhelmed by the onslaught of MNCs, give up;
   *(ii)* If you cannot fight, join them. Start collaboration and partnerships; or
   *(iii)* Use the long industrial and entrepreneurial experience and find strategies for survival and growth.

9. Nursing the infant and protecting the child phases of Indian Industrialization are over, freeing of adult is on. Life for the adults will be far more different and complex in the coming decades.

**Advice to Government**

10. Our first advice is to formulate a competition policy for India. We have overplayed the fear of foreign competition. We keep hearing about competition from abroad, level playing field and all that. But India does not have a competition policy for Internal competition of which foreign competition is only a small component.
11. We need to remove barriers to entry and exit. Nowhere in

the world entrepreneurs are prevented from closing a business. In India it takes years to close down a company.

12. We need to have entry policy which makes life easier for entrepreneurs starting their enterprises. Rules and Regulations and formalities will need to be simplified.
13. Fear that if we allowed easy exit, it will lead to unemployment is totally wrong. Take the example of America. Number of closures every year is more than compensated by number of them starting new ventures. There is no exit restriction, yet they have lowest unemployment.
14. Similarly, small scale industries in our country has relatively free exit. Experience of the SMEs shows that employment growth in unorganised sector is higher than the employment growth in organised sector. Therefore, sooner we accept the free entry and free exit policy as part and parcel of competition policy, the more benefit we will derive.

**Advice to Entrepreneurs**

15. Accept change, wake up, you will have no more government to blame. Next ten years will see government becoming less significant in the operation of Industries/business survival of the fittest is here, you recognise it sooner the better for you.
16. There is no alternative but to accept the fact that global competition is here. New kind of competition, new kind of technology, new kind of business organisations are here. Business management had changed. Instead of being frightened by the uncertainty accept it as an opportunity. Those who can exploit this situation will survive.
17. Build teams, i.e., face delegation and leadership crisis. Change your management style, acquire new knowledge, discipline yourself from old practices, retrain yourself.
18. Training or Retraining is a necessity which large number of entrepreneurs are beginning to feel. But unfortunately a fairly large number of them have not woken up. But next five years will see that you got to retrain yourself because you need new knowledge and discipline yourself. Old habits of physical check, supervision and lack of trust will not work.

**Advice to Bankers**

19. Financial Reforms are creating a situation where more and

more banks are less and less inclined to finance small scale industries. Five years back you could be a young entrepreneur, but five years from today you may not get money, because bankers have been asked to become financially viable. Gradually priority sector lending will disappear which means small, young, new entrepreneurs might find it difficult to get financial assistance. Our first advice to bankers is that small is still beautiful. It is a breeding ground of entrepreneurship. Small provides future tycoons. Most of today's impact making large entrepreneurs started from small.

20. Therefore, do not kill the golden goose. Special schemes to provide assistance to professionals, graduates, technical graduates, etc., will have to be introduced. These professionally qualified young entrepreneurs require fairly good amount of money. Therefore, special kind of financial assistance will have to emerge.
21. Venture capital will become very crucial.
22. Innovations are going to be important because of technology change. Indian industries will have to be innovative. All innovations cannot come from the Research laboratories of large companies. Most of the innovations come from small companies as USA has found out. They need venture funds to commercialise.

**Advice to Business Schools**

23. Business schools must introduce family business courses. It is a tragedy that very few business schools pay attention to management needs of family businesses.
24. Introduce development of soft skills competencies in the curriculum, build courses, cases, and content which can be useful for serving SMEs.

# 2

# Entrepreneurship and Economic Development

*—V. Lakshmana Rao*

"What is happening in the United States is... a profound shift from a "managerial" to an "entrepreneurial economy"—commented the doyen among the management experts Peter F. Drucker.

"From the stalls of a Moroccan market to the high-tech firms of California's Silicon Valley, entrepreneurship is transforming the globe the way that many who study the world have yet to grasp. Perhaps they were expecting a different sort of revolution, one in which the chariot of development—whether socialist or capitalist—would be drawn by the State. But as *The Culture of Entrepreneurship* shows, we are now witnessing the rise of an alternative development mechanism. In Latin America and Asia, Eastern Europe and Africa, a bottom-up revolution—what the Peruvian economist Hernanado Desot calls *El Otro Sendero* (The Other Path)—offers a new world for the dispossessed"—so writes Robert B. Hawkins Jr. in his foreword for the book *The Culture of Entrepreneurship.*

Thus, in both developed and developing countries entrepreneurship is a key to rapid economic development in the coming decades. With economic liberalisation initiated in 1991 in India, development of new innovative entrepreneurs has been receiving encouragement and support. The state-led development has been slowly giving way to private entrepreneurship-led development. With the advantage of hindsight we can say that State failed as an entrepreneur in India. The failure of many public sector enterprises and dismantling of mind boggling controls and regulations in India stand testimony to this. Even the sectors which are thought to be the preserves of the public sector (for example, infrastructure) are opened up for private initiative and entrepreneurial efforts. Through economic liberalization, environment conducive for new entrepreneurial development is being created and the process of development may receive a fresh fillip as a result of liberalisation and globalisation efforts in India.

With the serious, determined and sustained efforts taking place in developing economies including India and the "transitional economies" for rapid economic development, there is need for undertaking a detailed and searching analysis of different aspects of entrepreneurial role in harnessing the physical and human resources to generate forces of economic development. The factors which determine the supply of entrepreneurship, the rewards which assure entrepreneurs a sense of success, the conditioning external environment which nurtures innovative zeal, the socio-cultural factors which stimulate and not stifle entrepreneurial drive, and the capacity to adopt and adapt the store of technology available elsewhere are all aspects which deserve close scrutiny in order to understand the present state of development of a country. In this connection it is worth noting the suggestion made by Alexander Gerschenkoron—to speak of a general theory that may flatter a scholars ego but should offend his sense of realism. We are at all times condemned to deal with partial theories, some of them more and some of them less partial. Rather than following the will-o'-the wisp of a "general theory of entrepreneurship", the interested scholars should try to do what should have been done a long time ago; that is to say, to ask economically significant questions and in this way try to integrate entrepreneurial research with the main body of economic thought.

Development economists are concerned with, among others, the study of the human resources in general and entrepreneurship in particular. The study of the role of human resources in economic development will include aspects not only like educational levels and productive skills acquired by the labour force (which include all types of human resources) but also the aspects like social response to economic opportunity and readiness to undergo economic change on the part of the labour force. It is in the context of the latter aspects, socio-cultural besides economic factors assume considerable importance. Entrepreneurship is a form of human resource and it is as much influenced by the socio-cultural factors as any other.

Development economics tells us that the level and rate of economic growth depends on natural resource, physical capital accumulation, human resource development and technological progress, provided the socio-cultural environment is favourable to growth. Entrepreneurship is crucial for rapid economic development.

Discussing the circumstances which favoured the rise of entrepreneurs in Western industrial nations, Habbakkuk pointed to the key role played by innovative entrepreneurs and business leaders. Besides this, imitative entrepreneurship which involved a considerable degree of initiative and vigour also contributed substantially to the process of industrialisation. Among these entrepreneurs he finds differences in respect of both motives that inspired them and their background and objectives. While some were interested in quick speculative gains others had long run growth in their minds. But despite these differences, most entrepreneurs had certain common characteristics. A flair for identifying and seizing opportunities for profit, an eye for the possibility of new products, unexploited raw material supplies, untapped markets, the ability to devote their whole energies completely to attain their ends.

Most of these entrepreneurs, Habbakkuk explained, who owned and managed their enterprises in the early stages expanded their enterprises through ploughing back of profits. In the later stages of industrial development, technological as well as organizational changes favoured the growth of corporate enterprises. The spurt in the entrepreneurial activity needs an explanation as it is not common for human beings to sacrifice leisure and current consumption in order to accumulate saving of productive investment. Both the socio-religious features of the countries and high degree of social mobility go a long way in explaining large number of entrepreneurs devoting themselves to the task of economic development. No doubt there were differences among the western countries in this respect. While in the United States there were few competitors to business success as source of social prestige, in Western Europe land ownership, bureaucracy, the army and the professionals were all serious competitors to business for the services of the able men. "In western Europe therefore business has had to face greater competition for the able men than it has had to face in the USA." But in this respect, Europe is becoming more like America. *The wider therefore the circle from which a country draws its businessmen, the more likely it is to produce great entrepreneurs.*

During the last 50 years the circle from which India has been drawing its businessmen is widening, raising the hope that the entrepreneurial supply is gradually getting augmented. Chart 2.1 gives *Entrepreneurship : Sources of supply and motivation* drawing from different theories of entrepreneurship. The Indian studies reveal that in India entrepreneurship is both individual and group phenomenon. Tatas, Birlas, Sahu Jains as well as Ramoji Rao's and MVVS Murthy's adorn the Indian economic scene. There is a large unorganised sector in India accounting for more than 80 per cent of workforce. In 1993-94, unorganised sector accounted for 62.8 per cent of country's NDP. Unorganised sector thus represents significant potential of new entrepreneurship. In the present environment of economic liberalization and globalisation, the pace of entrepreneurial development may get accelerated.

Before concluding this paper I quote from Drucker who tells us that management is a "technology":

> "How do we explain, for instance, that all of a sudden there are such large numbers of people willing both to work like demons for long years and to choose grave risks rather than big organization security?. . . The vehicle of this profound change in attitudes, values, and above all, in behaviour is a 'technology'. It is called management. What has made possible the emergence of the entrepreneurial economy in America is new application of management:
>
> — to new enterprises, whether business or not, whereas most people until now have considered management applicable to existing enterprises only;
> — to small enterprises, whereas most people were absolutely sure only a few years ago that management was for the 'big boys' only;

**Chart 2.1**
**Entrepreneurship: Sources of Supply and Motivation**

| *Author* | *Entrepreneurial Phenomenon* | *Source of Entrepreneurial Supply* | *Motive Force of Trigging Mechanism* |
|---|---|---|---|
| 1. Schumpeter | Individual | Extraordinary individuals | Inherent urge to achieve success |
| 2. Weber | Status groups | Individuals Extraordinary | Religious belief Calvinist ethic |
| 3. Mc Clelland | Religious and social groups | Individuals with high-achievement | Child-rearing practices and climate |
| 4. Magen | Subordinated groups | Creative individuals in the society driven by a duty to achieve | 'Status withdrawal' and 'relative social blockage' |
| 5. Coahran | Individual | Society's 'modal' personality determined by its cultural values role expecptations and social sanctions | 'Social acceptance of entrepreneurial role |
| 6. Young | Homogeneous | 'Relative subgroups' (ethnic communities) occupational groups or politically oriented functions | Deviant view of the world strengthened by group solidarity |
| 7. Kunkel | Group | Operant conditioning procedures in a society | Reinforcing stimuli and average stimuli |
| 8. Hoselitz | Group | Culturally marginal groups | Gaining social recognition |

*Source:* V. Lakshmana Rao, *Industrial Entrepreneurship in India*, Allahabad: Chug Publications, 1986, pp. 85-86.

— to non-business (health care, education, and so on), whereas most people still hear "business" when they encounter the word 'management';

— to activities that were simply not considered to be 'enterprises' at all, such as local restaurants;

— and above all, to systematic innovation; to the search for and the exploitation of new opportunities for satisfying human want and human needs."

It is time for scholars in economics, commerce and management departments to conduct case studies of entrepreneurs in unorgànized sector covering different regions of the country.

**Notes and References**

Peter F. Drucker, *Innovations and Entrepreneurship*, New Delhi: Affiliated East-West Press Pvt. Ltd., 1984, p. 1.

Brigittee Barget (Ed.), *The Culture of Entrepreneurship*, New Delhi: Tata McGraw-Hill Company Ltd., 1991.

Alexander Gerschenkron, *The American Economic Review*, Paper and Proceedings, May, 1968, p. 98.

Among others E.E. Hagen, *The Economics of Development*, Homewood, Illinois : Richard D. Irwin, Inc., 1968.

On the basis of the degree of innovative zeal, propensity to introduce change, and qualities of leadership displayed entrepreneurs have been classified by Danhof into four distinct types. The first one is *innovating entrepreneurship* which is aggressive in experimentation and always ready for putting alternative possibilities into practice. The second is *imitative entrepreneurship*, distinguished by the preparedness to adopt successful innovations initiated by the innovating entrepreneurs. The third category is *Faian entrepreneurship*, characterised by great caution and scepticism, which introduces changes only when the non-introduction leads to loss. The fourth category is the *drone entrepreneurship* which is characterised by refusal to try new methods even at the risk of loss ("Observations on Entrepreneurship in Agriculture" in Cole (ed.) *Change and the Entrepreneur*, Cambridge : Harvard University Press, 1949, pp. 7-11.)

Habbakkuk, "The Entrepreneur and Economic Development" in I. Livingstone (ed.), *Economic Policy for Development*, Penguin Books, 1971, p. 39.)

*Ibid.*, p. 43 (emphasis is ours).

For a brief account of these studies are V. Lakshmana Rao, *Industrial Entrepreneurship in India*, Allahabad, Chugh Publication, pp. 70-74.

Peter F. Drucker, *Innovation and Entrepreneurship, op. cit.*, pp. 13-14.

# 3

# Entrepreneurship at X Roads

—*Prof. L. Venugopal Reddy,*
—*Prof. B. Ramachandra Reddy*
—*Prof. P. Seshanjaneyulu*

**Introduction**

In the 1950's every country, big or small, considered entrepreneurship as the surest way for quicker industrial and economic development. The developing countries like India have assigned greater significance for the development of entrepreneurship and encouraged the establishment of small scale industries to ease out the most burning problems of unemployment, capital shortage, etc., In fact, entrepreneurship has been considered as the panacia for many a socio-economic problems faced by the country.

During the planned era particular attention was paid to the establishment of more and more small scale, cottage and village industries by earmarking huge funds and also spelling out policy framework for a sustained development of this sector alongside the medium and large scale industries. However, all is not well with the small-scale industries. Many new industries were started year after year but have close down before realizing the fruits of entrepreneurship. The fruits of entrepreneurship are sour and bitter and enterprising people in the country did not relish them. In recent times, liberalization and globalization policy of the government dashed the hopes of some of the surviving running small scale industries and they are virtually pushed to the X roads for an eventual closure. "In this paper an attempt has been made to narrate the problems of many surviving small scale industries to draw the attention of the government on the future of entrepreneurship and small scale industries in the country."

**The Myth of Investment Ceiling and Excise Duty Concession**

The investment ceiling for small scale industries has been enhanced from time to time in view of the changing requirements. Recently, the Government has raised the investment ceiling up to Rs. 3 crores for small scale industries, but reduced to Rs. 1 crore subsequently. The small scale industries do need more capital for financing their assets as well as operations in an environment of open competition and free trade. The complexities in financing small scale industries are increasing day-by-day. The industries are not in a position to offer margin money and the burden has been the deadliest cause for sickness and closure of the small scale industries. Due to this problem several crores of rupees are blocked and the banks were not in a position to recover. Instead, the banks may advance short term loans at 4 per cent to 6 per cent rate of interest as in the case of other countries. This will help the industry to survive on a permanent basis. The greatest difficulty caused by the financial institutions is to start collecting the instalments even much before starting of the industry. In the case of final instalment of term loan, they deduct the interest accumulated from the date of advance and also some of the instalments, which had fallen due. As a result the entrepreneur again faces the shortage of finance. It is a fact that unless the unit reaches a break-even point, it is difficult to pay instalments to the financial institutions. Every officer from the financial institutions would like to implement the rules and try to collect the instalments without taking into consideration the performance of the unit whether it has reached a break-even point and is in a position to pay or not. The financial institutions often threaten to seize the unit if the instalment arrears are not paid. Right from day one the entrepreneur begins to work on a project with scuttled vialability. If the unit is made to commence production and if the financial institutions demand for payment of instalments there is no alternative except to siphoning the money from the working capital. This is done out of fear that the unit will be seized and the image of the unit would be tarnished.

### Collateral Securities

For financing term loan the banks insist on production of urban property and also other property as collateral security. If a person from joint family wishes to start an industry, the entire family may be appreciating his desire but may not be interested to give the entire property as collateral security but they would like to part some money for the benefit of the other family members as an entrepreneur. This is a natural phenomenon throughout India and then how it is possible for the entrepreneur to submit the collateral security to obtain loans from the Banks?

### The Problems of Working Capital Financing

When the enterprise grows, the need for working capital will become more. Though the banks know about the honesty and faithfulness of the entrepreneur, they still hesitate to finance the increased demand of working capital without further collateral security. This kind of attitude from the banks act as a major bottleneck for the growth of the units. Once the bank knows about the entrepreneurs capacity, it should liberally finance the required capital depending on the progress of the unit. In this connection the banks can adopt a new approach to safeguard the industry as well as to safeguard its investment in the industry. So far the entrepreneurs have been asking for the subsidized rate of interest from the financial institutions as well as Working Capital from banks but now the Government should come forward to subsidize the entire loan to safeguard the industry. This will help the government by way of indirect benefits to the exchequer and help to solve the unemployment problem and increase the G.D.P. of the Nation.

### Loopholes of ISI

As the world is changing towards quality there are many companies obtaining licenses from *Bureau of Indian Standards* and maintaining the quality. But unfortunately there are many loopholes in the functioning of this department. This has been encashed by the unscrupulous people by adopting various methods of cheating the public. ISI Certification is obtained from the offices at State Capitals. Therefore, the department checks the products for ISI license that are manufactured only in a particular state. This is an open secret and therefore, substandard products from other states with ISI mark but of a very substandard quality will be flooded at cheaper rates creating an obstacle to real quality conscious entrepreneurs. For example: A unit holding ISI license at Delhi supplies spurious materials with ISI mark in A.P. The department is helpless, once the product goes into other states no ISI Department can take the sample and check the quality standards.

As everyone is aware the distributors, dealers and middle man are attracted towards products with cheaper rates with a quality mark. Most of the purchases by the government departments are made by tender wherein it would be mentioned that the materials should be marked with ISI, but not bothered to test the quality. Tender means to quote the lowest rate and, therefore, the spurious materials with ISI mark will be infiltrated to the detriment blocking the products of genuine quality conscious entrepreneurs. In a global market competition it is the duty of the government to check the products wherever they are available in India and be tested. It is only then uniform standard products will be available throughout the country.

**Sales Tax**

When the world is trying to remove global barriers, why do we have restrictions to send a consignment with a proper way bill, etc. Once the gate pass of the Central Excise is given, there is no need of a document being accompanied by a way-bill. Sometimes, the way bill will not be available and the unit holder has to run around the department for procuring way bill. If the unit holder has not paid the tax dues, it is difficult to get the way bill and at certain times he may not be in a position to despatch the goods, thus foregoing the sales for that particular month. The postponement of the despatch due to the problem of way bill will reduce at least two times of turnover of every unit in every year. Furthermore, the unit, which plans to sell in various trades, has to submit a 'C-Form' for the goods sold to a dealer in the outside state. In general the dealer will not submit the C-Forms immediately but they will take their own time. There is certainly inordinate delay in procuring C-Forms from the dealers. It is impracticable for any manufacturer to produce all the C-Forms from the dealers, who are situated in different states, in different locations, prior to assessment. It is laborious for a unit holder to keep a track on the C-Forms and it leads to a lot of corruption both at the dealers side and manufacturers side. At the same time if any penalty is levied, the unit holder will be paying out of his hard-earned profits. The factory also contributes to the sickness of the units. The Government may respond to this issue and remove the C-Forms and allow the manufacturers to sell their products anywhere in the country. This system will help the manufacturers to plan the sales and organize their marketing efforts.

**Excise Duty Concession**

The object of Excise duty concession is to mitigate some of the problems of SSI units and to leave the industry in a reasonable level of profit. However, the raise in the level of excise duty from Rs. 30 lakhs to 50 lakhs is in no way matching the raise in investment level for SSI units. The investment level has been increased to 1 crore which means that the entrepreneur should make a turnover of 3 to 4 crores to achieve a break even point, but the parady is that the excise duty exemption is given up to 50 lakhs and 5 per cent up to 1 core turnover. What is the fate of units which have exceeded the 1 crore turnover. Since the excise duty is so high some of the units which are capable of producing more than 1 crore are not venturing to do so. The excise duty must be made to automatically apply for a capital turnover of 4 to 5 times in order to encourage the small scale sector. It is only then the industry will be in a position to undertake expansion, replacement and renewal, etc.

At a time when the government has opened the flood gates to Global marketing it should graciously remove excise duty barriers and help the SSI units to compete with global products and allow the entrepreneur to develop the industry.

# 4

# New Entrepreneurship Development: The Problems in Project Promotion and Financing

*—Dr. S. Moharana*

The pace and pattern of industrial development of an economy depends on the availability of adequate funds for investment and the supply of large pool of dynamic and result oriented entrepreneurs who can perceive the investment opportunities, organise resources to set up and successfully run the industrial units. A country may possess abundant and inexhaustible natural and physical resources, necessary machinery and capital equipment, but unless there are people who can combine these resources in right proportion, set the task and seek to its accomplishment, the nation cannot make rapid strides towards economic and social advancement. It has been rightly said that development or under-development is basically the reflection of development or under-development of entrepreneurship in the society.

During the Nineties, the Indian economy has been witnessing unprecedented changes. The move towards economic liberalisation and globalisation aiming at improving the productivity and efficiency of the sectors of the economy and making it internationally competitive is slowly paying dividends. The deregulation and delicencing process coupled with the withdrawal of the state from many economic activities have opened out a large number of business opportunities for private entrepreneurs. In order that the liberalisation policy of the Government succeed, it is essential that the base of entrepreneurship in the country is expanded and diversified both in the urban and rural areas. This would help not only in accelerating the pace of industrial development but also generate more and more employment opportunities, reduce regional imbalance and concentration of economic power and lead to all round economic growth comparable to other developed countries.

**Development Bank and Entrepreneurship Development**

The Post-Independent period has witnessed the creation of a network of development financing institutions, both at the national level as well as at the state level. These development banks promote industrial development by providing medium and long-term capital requirements of new and existing enterprises. In this sense, they act as the gap fillers in the capital market. For a long time, these DFIs functioned with development and achievement of socio-economic goals as their primary objective and profit making as their secondary objective. There has been some changes in the approach of these institutions in the post liberalisation period. Instead of a quantitative expansion, now they are more concerned with qualitative expansion of credit facilities. Instead of just development, they are now aiming at sustainable development.

The supply of entrepreneurship on an economy influences the level of business of a development bank and in turn is influenced by the business of a development bank. In a traditional economy like ours, the DFIs not only provide financial assistance to the existing entrepreneur but also induces the potential entrepreneurs to enter the entrepreneurial line by offering them a variety of financial and non-financial incentives and some times at some cost to the nation.

**New Entrepreneurship**

During the last four and half decades of their existence, the DFIs have tried to diversify the existing entrepreneurial base by creating new entrepreneurs from non-traditional sources. It has often been observed that in all economies, there are some specialised group of persons who more often go for industrial ventures in preference over other secured jobs. These persons normally come from the dominant business castes or communities. Because of their financial soundness, family background and business experience, they most often corner a major portion of different benefits provided by the Government to the entrepreneurs. However, for the purpose of accelerating the pace of economic development, new entrepreneurs should come not only from the few traditional sources but also from large number of non-traditional sources.

In addition to technical entrepreneurs, potential entrepreneurship also exists among a large group of persons who are employed in some organisation or have higher educational qualifications but remain unemployed or partly employed. Many DFIs have formulated different schemes for these types of persons who are otherwise known as "First Times" or "First Generation Entrepreneurs". The rationale behind the schemes for the FGEs is that many employees in industry and commerce, workers, supervisors, merchants, salesmen and other educationally qualified persons have latent talent and desire or capacity to be self-employed.

**Risks and Costs of New Entrepreneurship Creation**

Experience of developing new entrepreneurship in many economies have shown that even after providing all the required facilities, the rate of failure among new entrepreneurs is relatively high. Motivating the potential entrepreneurs from non-traditional sources is fraught with many social and personal risks. There are basically four types of risks taken by the persons:

(*a*) Financial Risk: Can the person afford to lose his investment?

(*b*) Career Risk: Can he return back to his previous job or career?

(*c*) Family and Social Risk: In case of failure, how will it affect his family and social reputation?

(*d*) Psychic Risk: How much afraid is he of Social failure?

Besides the personal risk of the entrepreneur, the financial institutions also take unduly high risk by financing new entrepreneurs at a very low margin and at liberal terms and conditions, thereby reducing the stake of the entrepreneurs. Some critics observe that in a resource shortage economy, providing liberal finance to these types of inexperienced persons at a very high risk is a direct cost to the economy and should be avoided. However, the Gujarat experiment conducted during the 70's, where 100 per cent finance was provided to new and technical entrepreneurs at very liberal terms, proved that this may be a short-term cost to the economy but in the long run, the expansion and diversification of the entrepreneurial base brings much more benefit.

**Entrepreneurial Problems: An Appraisal**

New entrepreneurs face a variety of problems during the promotion, financing and regular operation of the units. Some of these problems are created by the entrepreneur himself, some are due to the restrictive policies of the financial and development institution and still some others are created due to factors which are beyond the control of the entrepreneurs and the institutional agencies. The problems confronted by the entrepreneurs, if not taken care of in time, may convert the viable unit into a sick unit.

Instead of providing all the necessary ingredients for the successful operation of the units at concessional terms and conditions, Government is of the opinion that creating a conducive climate through the provision of adequate infrastructural support is its primary responsibility. It is the entrepreneur who should take the real initiative in sharing and operating the unit without much depending on concessional assistance of the Government agencies. However, this policy can not be made applicable to SSEs which are the breeding ground of new enterprise and therefore need a preferential treatment.

In order to get a practical insight into the problems of the new entrepreneurs in the small scale sector, a study of 48 units promoted by new entrepreneurs in Dhenkanal and Balasore districts of Orissa was undertaken during the year 1995. All the units were assisted by OSFC for term loan and by commercial banks for working capital loan. The units were engaged in manufacturing different types of products like handlooms, fabrication, chemicals, paperboard, ceramics, electrical parts, servicing, plastic bottles, food products, wood products, computer parts and consumer durables, assembly units. Of the

48 entrepreneurs, 4 had agricultural background, 18 business/ trade background, 16 were employed in technical and non-technical areas, 10 entrepreneurs had technical and others non-technical qualification but were unemployed or partly employed prior to entering into the industry. 26 entrepreneurs had no EDP training whereas 22 had EDP or some other type of industry exposure training of short duration.

The selection of the units was made through purposive sampling method and with the advice of the officers of OSFC and the state level financial institution. All the units had minimum operating life of approximately 4 years. There was a continuous default of principal and interest from all these units to OSFC for at least two consecutive instalments by 1995. All the units were in running condition.

The initial problems confronted by the new entrepreneurs can be analysed under two broad heads.

*(i)* problems during pre-investment phase and
*(ii)* problems during project implementation stage.

**Problems During Pre-Investment Phase**

Identification of viable investment opportunity is the first step in successful entrepreneurship. According to Murphy, the golden key to success is "Get into right business at the right time". However, an opportunity is viable only when it has been properly appraised with respect to marketability of the product, technical soundness, financial viability and managerial competence. It has often been observed that personal and emotional attachment of the promoter plays a major role in influencing his decision on the investment project. The Principle of compatibility of the project with the promoter and its viability is completely ignored. This type of wrong decision about product proposal creates a host of other problems for the entrepreneur and the financial institution at the later stages. Either the project report is prepared by some outside agencies to suit the requirement of the institution or pressure tactics adopted during the appraisal stage to influence the investment decision of the institutions. Sometimes, the institution takes the investment decision very reluctantly and after incorporating many hard and unrealistic conditions in the letter of intent which further increases the chances of sickness of the unit, primarily due to delay in compliance of such conditions.

Another problem during the pre-investment stage is the selection of a proper location for the project. In a majority of cases, the location decision were made on purely non-business grounds like nearness to home, availability of cheap land and investment subsidy for locating units in the backward regions. Obviously when financial incentives like subsidies, grant and concessions are available, the entrepreneur has hardly any option in the matter. However, this has proved to be a cause in disguise for most of the entrepreneurs, because of their decision to locate units at uneconomical sites. Another attraction of the investment subsidy for the entrepreneur during the promotion stage is the practice of considering subsidy as a part of promoter's contribution. At the time of project formulation, the entrepreneurs in their eagerness to minimise their contribution, opt for an area eligible for these concessions and commit themselves to an eternal handicap.

Preparation of project report after considering all internal and external factors is a serious problem for most of the new entrepreneurs. Of the 48 units, 36 units confessed that they had not conducted any detailed study of the market for the product but had depended entirely on the estimates of demand and supply on the basis of market reports prepared by various Government and semi-Government agencies or consultancy houses. This casual attitude at the promotional stage about the market potential proved to be very costly for them during the operational stages.

An objective appraisal of the project by the financial institution is essential for ensuring success of the project in the later stages. After an indepth study of the proejct reports and on the basis of discussions with the financial institution officials, it was observed that in many cases, the entrepreneurs through their malpractices during the promotion stage, intentionally force the units to become sick. Some of the entrepreneurs with business/ trade background were found to possess the "trader attitude" and were guided by their motive of making a fast buck. They resorted to different types of malpractices right from the promotional stage. The important ones are inflating the project cost and obtaining under the table commission from the suppliers of capital goods. This practice of inflating the project cost with or without the connivance of the officials without any corresponding increase in the earning capacity affect the BEP, debt servicing capacity, ROI and ultimately lead the unit to sickness.

**Problems During Project Implementation Stage**

While a wrong selection of project make the unit born sick, the problems during implementation phase turn a good project into a sick project. For new entrepreneurs, who lack industrial experience, implementation of a project becomes a pretty difficult task due to the need for simultaneous co-ordination of various non-related activities.

Obtaining quick disbursement of term-loan from the financial institution, arrangement of machines, and machine parts, civil construction, recruitment and training and personnel arrangement of required amount of working capital, procurement of new materials, power connection, making initial arrangement for marketing the product, etc., all need to be looked after by the entrepreneurs. Time factor is very important during project implementation stage. All the above activities need to be completed within a specific time period to avoid time and cost over run. The survey of the SSI units showed that all the entrepreneurs had faced a multiple of problems during the project implementation stage. The problems related to technical aspects like plant layout, procurement of machinery and components, negotiation and contracting, construction, recruitment and training, purchase of raw materials, power, etc. Besides, timely sanction of term loan and working capital continues to be a major problem with the majority of the entrepreneurs.

**Problem of Finance**

Among all the problems, the delay in arranging finance was experienced by a majority of the entrepreneurs. Working capital arrangement was found to be more difficult than arrangement of term loan. About 66 per cent of the units were not satisfied with the quantum of the loan and the procedural formalities. According to them the procedures are time consuming and cumbersome and some amount of loan money is required to be spent in satisfying the officials. While the gap between loan applied and loan sanctioned was 25 per cent on the average for term loan, it was more than 40 per cent in respect of working capital loan.

Among the units which could not procure the required amount of term loan, 12.5 per cent said they had to cut the size of the project, 50 per cent managed the extra fund from their own sources and 38.5 per cent borrowed from other sources. The general complaint of the entrepreneurs against both the commercial banks and OSFC related to the rate of interest, moratorium period, mode of repayment, lack of adequate information about the various schemes, terms and conditions of the sanction letter, multiplicity of documents, security stipulation and corruption.

It may also be stated here that the institutional assistance calls for fulfilment of certain terms and conditions which most often leads to the delay. A discussion with the official of the OSFC regarding the delay, reveals that the casual attitude and lack of prior knowledge of the entrepreneur regarding the normal terms and conditions of the sanction too often leads to the delay. According to OSFC, the non-compliance of the principal disbursement conditions indicates that management is not willing to submit to institutional discipline. The undue delay in getting licences approvals/sanctions from appropriate authorities also causes delay.

**Overrun in Project Implementation**

Because of a variety of problems, all the 48 units in the survey experienced a longer gestation period than estimated and consequently the time overran. Delays in project implementation leads to cost escalation due to increase in the prices of various cost components. In case there is cost escalation, the extra time taken to arrange the additional finance leads to time escalation.

**Time Overrun**

The range of time escalation among the sample units varied between 0-3 months to more than 12 months. The extent of time escalation was found to be higher in respect of entrepreneurs with service and educational background in comparison to those with business and trade background. However, the difference does not appear to be very significant. This leads us to conclude that most of the units set up by the new entrepreneurs are not free from time overrun.

As regard the causes of time overrun, both external and internal factors were responsible for it. External factors like natural calamities, infrastructural bottlenecks, strikes and lockouts in the factory of the machine supplier, etc., are beyond the control of the entrepreneurs. However, one should be more concerned about those controllable internal factors like lack of experience, inefficiency in co-ordination of diverse activities and inadequate knowledge of production and other technical matters causing delay in implementation. Among the sample units, the delay in procurement of finance, delay in procurement of plant and machinery and delay in getting clearances/approvals, etc., from various government/semi-government agencies were considered as the three most important factors causing delay in majority of projects. Besides, delay in electricity connection, delay in procurement of raw materials, technical problems during installation and trial production also contributed to the delay in respect of many units.

**Cost Overrun**

Cost overrun means additional financial burden on the promoter which most of the time passed on to the financial institution, in spite of the existence of a clause in the sanction later making it mandatory for the entrepreneur to bring in the additional fund from his own source in case there is a cost escalation. It may also be stated here that the project cost prepared by the financial institutions invariably includes the last item i.e., provision for contingencies which is normally estimated at 10-15 per cent of all the fixed costs.

In respect of 32 units, this provision was not found to be sufficient and the projects had to face cost escalation ranging from 5 per cent to more than 25 per cent of the project cost. The extent of cost escalation was found to be more or less same with different types of entrepreneurs. However, among all the projects started by the entrepreneurs with educated unemployed background had relatively higher cost overrun in comparison to others.

Higher construction cost, price rise of the machinery and

components due to delay in placing the orders, imposition of additional duties, under-estimation of preliminary and pre-operative expenses, changes in government policy were found to be some of the important reasons causing cost escalation. When there is cost overrun, the newly setup units only have to shoulder heavier problems. Further, the increase in pre-operative and pre-production expenses upset the working capital arrangements. As regards the impact of the cost escalation, 12 units felt that it had significant adverse impact on the financial performance of their units, for 26 units, it had only moderately adverse impact and for 20 units it had very insignificant impact or no impact.

**Financial Institution's Role in Project Promotion**

It is often felt that the success or failure of the enterprise is largely dependent among other factors on the policies and procedures of the development financing institutions. In the present day liberalised market environment, there is too much importance on productivity, efficiency and competitiveness. As a result, most of the savings of the society are being channelised to the profitable and large size industrial units. Banks and many large Financial Institutions are also showing a distinct preference to the large customers while sanctioning loan. In this highly competitive world, new entrepreneurship cannot be created unless the liberalised financing policy of DFIs, especially at the state level continues. Besides, there is need for a distinct change in their lending policies and practices so that only viable units started by the new entrepreneurs received the assistance. Some to the important areas which need a relook at the institution level are stated below :

***(a) Appraisal of New Entrepreneurs***

The institutions should very seriously think of giving more importance to the selection of right type of characteristics like risk taking, integrity, innovativeness, dynamism, etc. In comparison to other areas of appraisal, there is a laxity in the appraisal of the entrepreneur himself by many state level financial institutions. A system of screening should be developed whereby the non-serious entrepreneurs who have objective of diverting the funds of the unit and becoming rich at a short period of time at the cost of units are eliminated.

### *(b) Absence of Up-to-date Project Profiles*

Too often the decision of the new entrepreneur to enter or not to enter a line of activity is influenced by the advice of the financial institution officials or by the project profiles maintained by them which may not be very up-to-date. In case the assumptions in respect of marketing and technical study in the project go wrong, the units face a variety of problems. It is, therefore, necessary that the institutions maintain up-to-date project profiles which will be highly beneficial to the new entrepreneurs in the small scale sector.

### *(c) Weak Monitoring*

In most of the cases, the institutions show more seriousness in the appraisal and sanction of the proposal than in the monitoring stage. It is essential that during the project implementation stage the institutions should closely monitor the progress of the unit, to check diversion of funds, to ensure that the unit confirm to all the parameters in the project report, to safeguard the security of its own funds, to check the time and costs over-run and to clear all obstacles in the smooth implementation of the project. A close monitoring system is beneficial to both—the institution and to the unit. Thus the incidence of sickness among the new units, can be greatly reduced through an effective monitoring system.

### *(d) Quality of Loans Appraisal*

In many cases Loan Appraisal is done in a very stereotyped manner filling in some standardised forms and computing some selected ratios. Appraisal is both an art as well as a science. The creative part of the appraisal becomes faulty and the project sick. There is an urgent need to up-date the skills of the officers with respect to appraisal so that only viable units are selected and possibility of success of the new units goes up.

### *(e) Target Oriented Approach to Lending*

In their zeal to push up the assistance figures, sometimes, state level financial institutions adopt a target oriented approach in sanction and disbursement, this target oriented approach to lending is largely responsible for the setting up of a large number of unviable industrial projects and or assisting persons who do not have any of entrepreneurial qualities, the final result is the creation of a large number of born sick units. This approach has changed a lot during the last few years. It is felt that instead of fixing targets for sanction and disbursement, the approach should be about creating a conducive environment and motivating the serious entrepreneurs to start their own venture.

### *(f) Co-ordination Between DFIs and Commercial Banks*

In spite of the single window approach to lending and the universal concept of banking, the DFIs and the commercial banks continue to emphasise on their own line of lending, viz., financing of fixed assets and current assets respectively. Many new entrepreneurs complain about absence of any effective co-ordination between the banks and SFC. These two institutions do not trust each others reports. As a result the entrepreneur and his project report is appraised twice both at the level of SFC (for sanction of term loan) and the level of banks (for sanction of working capital). This consumes a lot of time and results in cost and time overrun. An effective co-ordination and free flow of information between banks and financial institutions not only reduces sanctioning time but also ensures effective monitoring of the end use of funds both in the fixed assets and current assets.

## Conclusion

The industrial development is largely dependent on the availability of a large number of innovative and dynamic entrepreneurs. The type of entrepreneurship can only be developed in the small scale sector which is the breeding ground for new entrepreneurs. The financial institutions at the state level have all along been trying to develop new entrepreneurship from both the traditional and non-traditional source by offering a variety of financial and non-financial incentives at very liberal terms and conditions. Over the years, there has been a quantitative expansion in the entrepreneurial base but this has led to a large number of sick units in the State Financial Corporations portfolio. During the post liberalisation period, with the shift in emphasis from quantity to quality, the approach of the institution has also changed from provision of cheap finance to provision of finance at the normal rate to the deserving entrepreneur and ensuring successful operation of the industrial units. In the present article the major problems encountered by the new entrepreneurs during promotion and financing of the industrial projects have been discussed on the basis of above discussions.

The following suggestions are being made to ensure that problems faced by the entrepreneurs during promotion and financing are reduced to the minimum.

*(i)* Selection of entrepreneurs for the Entrepreneur Development Programme and also for financial assistance by the institutions should be done on a scientific basis so that non-serious entrepreneurs are eliminated from the process.

*(ii)* EDPs should be less academic and more practical oriented, so that the participants are able to pick-up the qualities needed to face the various hurdles in the real life situation.

*(iii)* Up-to-date and entrepreneur specific project profiles should be maintained at the financial institution level so that the new entrepreneurs in these project areas become successful. Entrepreneurs who approach the institutions with unviable or saturated projects should be discouraged.

*(iv)* The institutions should register a list of consulting agencies who can render the necessary help to the new entrepreneur at reasonable cost.

*(v)* The approach in lending should shift from providing concessional finance to providing need based finance at normal rates of interest.

*(vi)* Some relaxations may be provided in the area of moratorium period, mode of repayment, security stipulation, etc., so that unanticipated problems affecting finance can be taken care of by the entrepreneurs.

*(vii)* The target oriented approach in entrepreneurship creation should be completely dispensed with. Entrepreneurship cannot be created by just providing finance. The entrepreneurship development policy should henceforth stress more on training, viable project preparation and providing suitable environment rather than only financial incentives.

*(viii)* There should be a single window approach to clear all problems, licences, approvals, etc., at one place.

*(ix)* The proposals for both term loan and working capital loan should be jointly appraised by SFCs and banks to eliminate delay and need for joint appraisal of projects and entrepreneurs.

*(x)* Assistance cell be set up at the financial institutions level to look after the problems of the problem units. The unviable units should be closed and assets disposed off without delay. The entrepreneurs should be offered some other alternative opportunity if it is clear that the unit has become sick for reasons beyond their control.

*(xi)* The officers of the institutions should be trained at periodical intervals to up-date their appraisal skills. Sufficient number of inhouse training programmes be conducted on a continuing basis to make them aware of the internal and external changes taking place in respect of different industries.

*(xii)* Maximum emphasis be given to supervision and monitoring of the assisted units. It should not be a stereotyped task. Rather individual care should be taken to analyse the progress reports and other informations received from the unit so that problems can be detected at the early stage. Periodical visits should also be conducted at regular and irregular intervals to collect on the spot information about the operation of the units.

## Reference

1. Singh L.P., "State Incentives and Growth of Small Entrepreneur in India" in *Entrepreneurship Development In India* (Ed.) Samiuddin, Mittal Publications, New Delhi, 1989, p. 143.
2. *IDBI,* "Development Banking in India", Bombay, 1980, pp. 3-4.
3. Patel, V.G. "Innovations in Banking; the Gujarat Experiment" in *IDBI,* Bombay, 1981, p. 4.
4. Sue Birley, "An Opportunity—But is it Worth It?" in *Mastering Enterprise,* Business Standard, New Delhi.
5. Patel V.G., *op.cit.*
6. Murphy, Thomas P., "A Business of Your Own : How to Select, Finance and Start it Successfully", McGraw Hill, New York, 1956, p. 4.
7. Rayaguru, B.P., "Symptoms and Signals of Sickness in Pre-investment and Investment Phase", *IED,* Govt. of Orissa, Bhubaneswar.
8. Clifton, David S. and Fyffe, David E., "Project Feasibility Analysis", Wiley Publications, New York, 2977, p. 4-5.
9. *IDBI,* "Time and Cost Overrun of IDBI Assisted Units", Research and Planning Deptt., Bombay, 1984, p. 2.
10. Kuchhal, S.C., "Problems in Promotion and Financing of New Projects", *IIM,* Ahmedabad, 1982, p. 18.

# 5

# Entrepreneurship and Economic Liberalisation: The Case of Indian Coffee Industry

*—Dr. M. Panduranga Vithal*

## Background

"The entrepreneur" said the French Economist J.B. Say around 1880, "shifts economic resources out of an area of higher productivity and greater yield." But Say's definition does not tell us who this "entrepreneur" is. And since Say coined the term almost two hundred years ago, there has been total confusion over the definitions of "entrepreneur" and "entrepreneurship."

Every practice rests on theory, even if the practitioners themselves are unaware of it. Entrepreneurship rests on a theory of economy and society. The theory sees change as normal and indeed as healthy. And it sees the major task in society and especially in the economy as doing something different rather than doing better what is already being done. This is basically what Say, two hundred years ago, meant when he coined the term entrepreneur. It was indeed as a manifesto and as a declaration of dissent. The entrepreneur upsets and disorganizes. As Joseph Schumpeter formulated it, his task is "creative destruction".

Joseph Schumpeter was the first major economist to go back to Say. In his classic *Dic theorie der Wirtschaftlichen Entwicklung*

(The theory of Economic Dynamics), published in 1911, Schumpeter broke the traditional economics—far more radically than John Maynard Keynes was to do twenty years later. He postulated that dynamic disequilibrium brought on by the innovating entrepreneur, rather than equilibrium and optimization, is the 'norm' of a healthy economy and the central reality of economic theory and economic practice.

Entrepreneurs see change as the norm and as healthy economy. Usually, they do not bring about the change themselves. But—and this defines entrepreneur and entrepreneurship—the entrepreneur always searches for change, responds to it, and exploits it as an opportunity. The first four sources of systematic innovation to monitor an innovative opportunity lie within the enterprise, whether business or public-sector institution or within an industry or service sector. They are basically symptoms. These four sources are:

1. The unexpected—the unexpected success, the unexpected failure, the unexpected outside event;
2. The incongruity—between reality as it actually is and reality as it be assumed to be or as it "ought to be";
3. innovation based on process need;
4. Changes in industry instructure or market structure that catch everyone unawares.

The Indian coffee industry offers an exemplary lesson in entrepreneurship and economic development.

**The Indian Coffee Industry: An Introduction**

It was in 1935 that the coffee planters led by Iver Bull of Conscoffee convinced the government to have a strategy to cope with the problems of coffee. Such an agency would ensure better price realisation to the growers and prevent any fall in the prices of coffee in the domestic market due to over supply. With the International Coffee Agreement in place, the growers badly needed a national level agency to deal with the quotas for exports. The result was the establishment of Coffee Board, a statutory body under the Coffee Act, 1942.

**Role of Coffee Board in Pre-liberalised Era**

Coffee was being marketed through a centralised pooling system for nearly half a century under the auspices of the Coffee Board. The Coffee Board itself came into existence at the request of the coffee growers who found it difficult to market their coffee in the post-war critical period. All the coffee was pooled as per the provisions of the Coffee Act, with the Coffee Board. Later, after curing and grading, coffee was marketed through a dual auction market system. That is, the pooled coffee was auctioned in two different auctions, one meant for international markets, where only exporters participated, and the other for domestic market, where the domestic traders participated. Coffee was exported as per the quotas allocated to India under the International Coffee Agreement in the first place. In case of exportable surplus, which was often the case, coffee as exported to countries, like the erstwhile USSR, with whom India had trade arrangements. Since coffee was regarded as a foreign exchange earner, the emphasis was more on exports. Supplies to domestic market were often regulated and domestic prices were kept low, by controlling the releases by the Board. The controlled releases of pooled coffee through regular auctions helped in maintaining an "average-price" realisation for the growers. Coffee Board provided all the marketing and infrastructural support required by the growers, curers, traders and exporters, thus creating a highly protected and paternalistic atmosphere. It also provided a very valuable research and extension support. The research department was especially well known for the release of high yielding and the disease resistant varieties. The field officers of the Board were considered true friends, philosophers and guide to the growers. The Board in effect had a virtual control over the total value chain.

**Mechanism for Price Realisation**

Under the pooling system, growers are credited with certain points depending upon the quantity and quality/grade of coffee pooled with Board. Payments were being made to growers out of the sale proceeds, in instalments after deducting the expenses on marketing operations. These payments were received over a period, which sometimes took even more than two years.

**Rationale for Deregulation of Coffee Marketing**

The International coffee agreement was discontinued in 1989

(reformulated in 1992 and will expire in 1999) primarily due to withdrawal of a major consuming country, the United States from the agreement. Thus, the international quota system came to an end. The surplus coffee above quota allocations produced in the country was earlier predominantly traded with the erstwhile USSR. With the disintegration of USSR, even this market arrangement needed a change. Once the Indian economy was liberalised in June 1991, a new market environment was created. Hence, the coffee growers saw an opportunity to exercise their option for market freedom. Thus, the juggernaut of market freedom started rolling with the introduction of an internal sale quota for the season in 1992-93.

### Constitution of the Indian Coffee Industry

Coffee all over the world is produced by small growers generally. In India, there are nearly 140,000 growers on the basis of land holdings of less than 10 hectares. They constitute 98 per cent of the growers. The remaining 2 per cent are large growers. The small growers contribute 60 per cent of the production and the large growers produce the remaining 40 per cent. The data regarding the distribution between small and large growers is given in Table 5.1.

**Table 5.1**
**Distribution Pattern of Holding in Different States**

| *Holding Pattern* | *Share of Production* | *Total number of Holdings* |
|---|---|---|
| Small Holdings less than 10 Hectares | 60% | 137643 |
| Large Holdings 10 Hectares | 40% | 2650 |

*Source* : Database on coffee, March 1998, Coffee Board.

India produces less than 3 per cent of the total world production. Nearly 70 to 75 per cent of the production is exported, as the domestic market never consumed beyond 20 to 25 per cent of the production.

### The Path of Market Freedom

There were suggestions for deregulation of coffee marketing in the pre-liberalised era. At least three major studies advised deregulation. The brief suggestions of these studies are:

***Indian Institute of Management, Ahmedabad, 1978***

- The Indian Institute of Management in its report (1978) suggested that besides Export Market, development of an expanded and stable domestic market is necessary which would require market development in non-traditional areas as well.
- Role of Coffee Board: The Board may continue the procurement and sale of coffee. The Board should market coffee aggressively in non-traditional areas. The Board can directly distribute coffee to consumers in non-traditional areas.
- Growers co-operatives to be set up, with the Board being a major share-holder to overcome limitations in terms of funds and required specialization other than in the areas of procurement and auctioning. This also would ensure that there are no conflicts of interests between coffee growers and that of the co-operative. Market development would require a large investment and the fruits of that would not be fully available to the Board unless the Board is involved in coffee processing and value addition especially in the area of coffee powder and instant coffee. This would ensure growers a fair share of consumers rupee.
- HSP could come into operation to protect the growers from the vagaries of price fluctuation.
- Complete deregulation could be considered. This would leave the development of the industry to market forces. The free competition, the result of completed deregulation may even develop a system of forward sale of standing corps.
- Development of appropriate co-operative institutions could be a long term solution to protect the interests of the small growers in particular and industry in general.
- Any changeover from the existing system should be in a phased manner so as to allow for creation of alternative institutional arrangements.

Considering the structure of this industry, the government of India deemed fit to deregulate in phases.

After many such deliberations, the industry decided to change gears to tread the promising path of free market with the allowance of an internal sales quota of 30 per cent to the growers in 1992-93. As per section 25 of the Coffee Act, all the coffee produced by registered estates in excess of the quantity specified in the Free Sale Quota (FSQ) allotted to that estate shall be delivered to the Board for inclusion in the surplus pool by the grower/curing establishment receiving the coffee from the estate. Growers could sell 30 per cent of their produce in the domestic market according to this policy. An enthusiastic response and fervent appeal for greater autonomy lead to the 50 per cent Free Sale Quota (FSQ) an year later. A simultaneous unprecedented increase in the international prices, on account of short supplies from Brazil due to successive frost, resulted in a pitched up demand for full marketing freedom.

Meanwhile the prices of coffee powder in domestic market increased considerably. For example, Robusta Cherry wholesale price moved from Rs. 37 per kg in 1993 to Rs. 90 in 1995 in Bangalore, from Rs. 39 to Rs. 94 in Mysore, from Rs. 39 to Rs. 98 in Madras, Rs. 40 to Rs. 101 in Hyderabad and from Rs. 41 to 110 in Vijayawada (all stations are important coffee consuming centres). The very sharp increase in the domestic powder price was obviously not welcome to the consumers within the country, used as they were, to subsidised prices earlier. A via media policy of 100 per cent free sale quota for small growers (10 hectares holding) and 70 per cent only for large growers was announced in April 1995.

The disparity between the international and domestic prices continued. Market intervention by the Board or any other agency did not materialise, though it was envisaged in the policy. In September 1996, 100 per cent free sale quota policy was announced. Thus, the marketing system experienced gradual but significant shift from single, large marketing operation to a complete open free market system. From 30 per cent ISQ in 1992-93 to 100 per cent FSQ marketing policy in 1996, there has been positive path of development.

### Challenge for Entrepreneurship Abilities of Coffee Growers

The main issue was whether the entrepreneurs of the coffee industry, mostly comprising of small growers would be able to handle the marketing freedom. It was doubted as they remained under protected umbrella of Coffee Board for more than fifty years without any exposure to nuances for marketing (result of only Coffee Board auctions without grower participation) and financial wisdom (result of delayed payments on the poist system), since the industry is excessively dependent on export market, it was doubted whether the growers will be able to handle the exporters directly. In spite of these doubts no attempt was made to design or define an alternative marketing system either by the policy makers or by the leaders of the industry. It is our hunch that probably everybody thought that the free market forces would allow the emergence of a new marketing system almost automatically.

Here was a major challenge for the entrepreneurial abilities of the coffee growers, traders, curors and exporters.

**Table 5.2**
**Coffee Production, Exports—Targets and Achievements**
*(In tonnes)*

| *Year* | *Production* | *Target Quantity* | *Achievements* |
|---|---|---|---|
| 1990-91 | 169726 | 100800 | 100110 |
| 1991-92 | 180000 | 120000 | 111452 |
| 1992-93 | 169395 | 120000 | 113602 |
| 1993-94 | 208000 | 150000 | 136690 |
| 1994-95 | 180100 | 150000 | 137395 |
| 1995-96 | 223000 | 150000 | 170990 |
| 1996-97 | 205000 | 150000 | 181295 |
| 1997-98 | 228000 | 165000 | 133153 |

*Source:* Database on Coffee, March, 1998, Coffee Board.

## Developments in the Liberalised Era

During the transition period, production has positively increased. The industry has also witnessed a steady growth in exports from 2.69 per cent share of world exports in 1988-89 to 4.07 per cent in 1995-96. Production and exports performance in quantity and value terms are presented in Tables 5.2 and 5.3. The export performance of the industry is presented in Tables 5.3 and 5.4.

**Table 5.3**
**Coffee Exports—Targets and Achievements (in value)**

| *Year* | *Target Value Rs. Crores* | *Achieved Value Rs. Crores* |
|---|---|---|
| 1990-91 | 280 | 278.89 |
| 1991-92 | 400 | 349 |
| 1992-93 | 400 | 381.31 |
| 1993-94 | 400 | 586.99 |
| 1994-95 | 675 | 1096.33 |
| 1995-96 | 1200 | 1527.16 |
| 1996-97 | 1500 | 1467.08 |
| 1997-98 | 1613 | 1265.87 |

*Source :* Data Base on Coffee, March 1998, Coffee Board

**Table 5.4**
**Achievements**

- Initiation of brands for pure coffee, instant coffee and other varieties of coffee.
- Establishment of Indian Coffee Marketing Co-operative Ltd. (COMARK) and enhancement of its activities discussed in detail (the next section).
- Progressive activities on the part of Coffee Board with respect to initiating discussions with exporters for promotion, conducting Brain Storming sessions regarding future role of the Board and future of the industry and a successful drive to make hotels and restaurants to train their people on how to improve the cup quality of made coffee.
- The research and extension departments have conducted a series of mass contact programm to advise growers on problems at the estate level.
- On the formation of Indian Coffee Trade Association (ICTA), besides the Board's auction centre, additional auction centres have also started functioning.

In sum, these developments indicate that the industry was trying to tackle economic liberalisation and looking for avenues for improvement.

**Indian Coffee Marketing Co-operative Ltd. (COMARK)**

With the liberalisation of coffee marketing, the growers of

**Table 5.5**
**Receipts of Coffee into the Pool 1984-85 to 1995**

| *Season* | *Quantity in Tonnes* |
|---|---|
| 1984-85 | 194565 |
| 1985-86 | 121916 |
| 1986-87 | 191647 |
| 1987-88 | 122275 |
| 1988-89 | 214271 |
| 1989-90 | 117480 |
| 1990-91 | 169328 |
| 1991-92 | 175682 |
| 1992-93 | 119240 |
| 1993-94 | 47221 |
| 1994-95 | 11236 |
| 1995-96 | 7415 |

*Source :* Database on Coffee, March 1998, Coffee Board.

Karnataka, Kerala and Tamilnadu felt the need of a marketing agency. The introduction of Internal Sales Quota System in 1991-92 by the Coffee Board left the coffee marketing efforts to the growers which made them to think of a solution that ensured the benefits of pooling system while improving on deficiencies of it.

**Performance**

Comark has registered a rapid growth in its network expansion and business turnover in a short period of 4 years. Comark has also taken a number of new initiatives to link the growers with the domestic and overseas coffee market. The procurement operations of Comark had grown substantially, by 89.60 per cent in quantity, by 35.60 per cent in value during the year 1995-96 as compared to 1994-95. The sales volume of coffee registered a growth of 23 per cent while sales realisation registered a growth of 45.80 per cent during 1995-96 over 1994-95. However, the financial performance of Comark, during the year 1995-96, came under severe pressure. This was due to the distortions created by Brazil frost in the international market. The international prices witnessed a consistent fall accompanied by volatility. The disparity between domestic and international prices further contributed to the losses.

*The Lessons Learned from the Operations*

1. The contracting pattern during the process of export of coffee is too rigid, and one cannot withdraw from the commitment even if one wishes to. This may prove counter productive in constantly volatile and falling price situation.
2. Comark has found it difficult to evolve a procurement system for export that would synchronise with daily changes in prices, eliminates uncertainties in procurement prices and meets with the requirements of taxation procedures.
3. Given the volatility of the market, the growers have obviously developed the tendencies to hold coffee stock when the prices are low and release the same at high prices.

**Establishment of COFIFED**

At the Second Asia International Coffee Conference held at Singapore in January 1996, India had suggested that there is a need for restructuring the Indian Coffee Industry providing leadership at three levels. At the top level there could be an apex catalytic agency to provide strategic leadership to the industry. Such a body could be either one representing all the major constituents of the industry or a restructed Coffee Board. Afterwards, there was an attempt to define the future role of the Coffee Board in a series of Brain Storming Workshops where most of the segments of the Coffee Industry participated. Further to this, a new organisation COFIFED was established.

The aims of the Federation was to develop the coffee industry, to promote, protect and represent the interests of the trade, promote consumption of Indian Coffee in the domestic and international markets and to develop and provide technical, commercial and scientific knowledge in respect of production, processing and marketing of coffee.

**Coffee Alternative Marketing System Study**

As a follow-up to these developments, the need for detailed study to explore the possibility of developing an alternative coffee marketing system was felt. The study was initiated by the Coffee Board and the Indian Institute of Plantation Management.

The objective of the study was to assess the impact of deregulation of coffee marketing. The purpose of the study was to explore the missing links in the deregulated marketing system in order to bridge the gap and strengthen the marketing scenario. The questions raised, for example, were like:

1. What should the new marketing system achieve?
2. Whether there was a better price realization to farmers ?
3. Should there be a role for the Coffee Board or any such governmental agency for market intervention or only a developmental role ?

*Major Findings of the Study*

The growers highlighted two advantages of the post-FSO marketing system:

*(i)* Higher price realization, and
*(ii)* Freedom to store and dispose of the commodity as per the demand.

They identified three major disadvantages of the post-FSQ marketing system:

*(i)* Price volatility leading to speculation and stock-holding.
*(ii)* Price manipulation by traders/agents, and
*(iii)* Dishonest trade practices.

These findings suggested the need for transparency and discipline in the marketing system. Two of the notable suggestions to improve the marketing system were one for standardization of quality parameters and the other setting up of any agency to enforce market discipline.

There was an urgent need to strengthen the critical links of the industry value chain.

Articulation about objectives of a marketing system;

The growers were able to articulate the objectives of the proposed coffee alternating marketing system as:

- Ensure stable prices,
- Maximize return to growers,
- Transparency in the transactions of internal traders and exporters with the growers,
- Inspire to improve the quality, and
- Ensure affordable price to domestic consumers.

**Path to Domestic Coffee Futures Exchange**

While one may agree with the presence of vacuum in the marketing system, the industry cannot shy away from the responsibility to develop an alternative system. It had ample opportunity of nearly 4 years to develop sustainable market linkages. However, this did not take place. As a result the aimed integration of domestic market with the international market and its consequent synchronization of the domestic and international prices remained an unfulfilled dream. The differences in the international and domestic prices over the last 3 years between August 1994 to the end of October 1996 was as low as Re. 1 and as high as Rs. 1939, for a 50 kg bag of Plantation. Arabica was as high as Rs. 550 while for Robusta Cherry-AB it was Rs. 963. This indicates that auction prices at home are not in line with the international prices. This indicates price volatility : There was a need for a price discovery mechanism which would

- Reduce price fluctuations.
- Match demand and supply, and
- Ensure the regularity to reduce impact of speculation.

The coffee alternative marketing system study threw up the concept of Domestic Coffee Futures Exchange. Coffee Futures Exchange of India Ltd. (COFEI) came into existence in the following phases:

- Concept of Domestic Coffee Futures Exchange December, 1996.
- Workshop on Domestic Coffee Futures Contract and setting up of an Industry Working Group, May 1997.
- Registration December 1997.
- Recognition March 1998.
- Mock Trading May 1998.
- Trading June 1998.
- Business till July 31, 1998; 2325 transactions in 32 days (2 hrs).

**Away from the Dependancy Syndrome**

It is said that there is no free lunch in a free market. Coffee growers have earned their marketing freedom. The growers met the entire cost of deregulation. They paid Rs. 20 crores out of the marketing pool funds to offer a golden handshake to 2000 of the 3000 employees of the Coffee Board. The growers proved a point here as this was the biggest and smoothest voluntary retirement scheme successfully implemented in any industry in India.

This entrepreneurial marvel was not restricted to the coffee growers in the traditional belts only. Even the tiny non-traditional coffee growers in Andhra Pradesh bravely faced the situation. They continued to produce, more even though in small increments, and marketed them successfully. Market reports indicate that they achieved a record production of 1,400 tonnes in this season in 30 years. A revenue of Rs. 15.5 crores was generated whereas the cost of production was about Rs. 6 crores. This helped the people in the tribal areas to move away from the "podu" cultivation as the coffee plantations offered employment throughout the year.

**Conclusion**

The coffee industry needs to plan and implement the following in the interest of the industry to gain from the entrepreneurial efforts put in so far after deregulation.

- Study the cost of operations to enable the industry to workout its cost competitive edge.
- Code of conduct for different players.
- Monitoring agency for enforcing the code of conduct.
- Detailing of quality requirements and setting quality centres.
- More modern auction centres at major coffee growing districts ensuring transparency and guaranteeing of transaction.
- Strengthen the domestic coffee futures exchange.
- More frequent business meets between different players in the coffee growing areas.
- More involvement of respective state governments.
- Requesting the Coffee Board for domestic as well as International generic promotions of coffee through coffee festivals.

Success of these recommendations will depend entirely on ensuring the "deregulation of attitude" by one and all constituents of the industry. It is heartening to note that efforts like setting up a Coffee Futures Exchange of India Ltd (COFEI) indicates the entrepreneurial strength of industry towards the development of an alternative Coffee marketing system. Such a strength promises a bright future for the Indian Coffee industry.

## References

1. Drucker, Peter F. (1991), *Innovation and Entrepreneurship,* Affiliated East-West Press Private Ltd., Chs. 1 & 2 (Excerpts).
2. Muthian S. (1993), *A Planting Century,* Affiliated East-West Press Pvt. Ltd., p. 120.
3. Panduranga Vithal, M. (1998), "Indian Coffee Industry, Emerging Scenario, After Deregulation." in Jayachandran, *et al.* (ed.), 1998, *Managing Economic Liberalisation in South Asia, Direction for the 21st Century,* Macmillan India Ltd., pp. 247-58.
4. *Ibid.*
5. Matthai, P. and Panduranga Vithal, M. (1997), *Alternative Coffee Marketing System Study Report.*
6. Panduranga Vithal, M. (1996), *New Development in Indian Coffee Industry for Better or Worse?* IIPM/WPS/9601.
7. *Op. cit.*
8. Matthai, P. and Panduranga Vithal, M. (1996), "Concept for a Coffee Futures Market in India," *The Economic Times,* December 19, p. 13.
9. *Business Line,* 18-5-1998.

# 6

# Role of Institutions in Entrepreneurship Development

*—Mrs. R. Vijaya*

A number of social scientists have contended that Entrepreneurship is the key variable which links the socio-cultural milieu with the rate of economic development. The emphasis has been shifted from the rate of capital formation to the growth of high level manpower such as entrepreneurs who have become the major determinants of economic growth. There has also been a wide recognition that the entrepreneurial development is essential not only to solve the problem of economic development but also to solve the problems of unemployment, unbalanced areas development, concentration of economic power and diversion of profits from traditional avenues of investment. The experiences from developing countries all over the world favour the hypothesis that entrepreneurship can be developed through planned efforts. It is possible to identify individuals in all communities, in rural and urban areas, among men and women with Entrepreneurial talent, to motivate and train them through properly organised programmes, to undertake with bearing innovative activities to raise the growth rate in industry as well as in service sector. The major hurdles impeding entrepreneurship in our country are lack of awareness regarding entrepreneurial opportunities, lack of proper training and motivation, financial constraints and certain operational and marketing problems. According to the modern writers entrepreneurship is a complex phenomenon to be developed and requires a systematic and disciplined approach. They have identified three phases in Entrepreneurship development. The initial phase of creation of awareness about entrepreneurial opportunities based on survey, the development phase of implementation of training programmes to develop motivation and managerial skills and the support phase providing infrastructural support and counselling to establish a new enterprise and develop the existing units. In order to guide the entrepreneurs in these phases and to meet their requirements the government has provided adequate institutional support and it may be well claimed to have achieved considerable success in this sphere. The institutional infrastructure of our country is vast and consists of institutions providing entrepreneurial awareness, organising entrepreneurship development programmes and motivation programmes providing financial support, dealing with marketing problems, providing consultancy and education in Entrepreneurship, conducting research in the area and so on and so forth. An attempt is made in this chapter to discuss the role of the important institutions in entrepreneurship development, to narrate the activities, schemes and programmes undertaken by these institutions to improve entrepreneurship in the country.

**Entrepreneurship Development Institute of India (EDI)**

EDI is not a profit organisation and an autonomous body set up in 1983, sponsored by the apex financial institutions, the IDBI, IFCI, ICICI and SBI. The Government of Gujarat pledged 23 acres of land on which stands the majestic campus.

EDI is a national resource institution committed to Entrepreneurship Education, training and research, striving to provide innovative training techniques, competent faculty support, teaching and training material, besides sharing benefits of inhouse research as well as experience in relevant sphere. EDI has been spearheading Entrepreneurship movement throughout the nation with the belief that entrepreneurs need not necessarily be born but can be developed through well-concerned and well-developed activities. EDI has linkages with a nationwide network of organisations and institutions commuted to entrepreneurship development. It is an inter-regional centre for entrepreneurship and investment training sponsored by United Nations Industrial Development Organisation and Government of India, a national facility for Science and Technology based entrepreneurial innovations sponsored by National Science and Technology Entrepreneurship Development Board, DST, Government of India and a member of Economic and Social Commission of Asia and the Pacific network of centres of excellence for Human Resource Development, Recruitment and Training.

The various trust areas of EDIs functions include entrepreneurship in education, performance and growth of existing entrepreneurs, micro enterprise and micro finance development, performance improvement of Entrepreneurship development organisation and EDP's, entrepreneurship environment and support system and research in entrepreneurship education and development.

Realising that Education is an apt medium to reach out to a wider section of society, Entrepreneurship in education is an important thrust area of the Institute. Under this area the programmes organised are Faculty development programmes for teachers of Engineering Colleges/Schools, summer camps for children and youth enabling them to imbibe the traits of a competent Entrepreneur and seminars and workshops for Educationists, planners, policy makers and administrators to chalk out a positive course of future action with respect to introducing entrepreneurship in education.

In order to address the growing demands for training on micro-credit delivery system management, rural marketing capabilities and inhouse financial management among GNOs, EDI has been organising skill development programmes on a continuous basis. These programmes have been specifically designed to address the needs/requirements of entrepreneurs trained under rural Entrepreneurship programmes, train extention workers of NGOs/VOs with skills to help rural youth in launching their micro enterprises, strengthen NGO personnel to manage their finance and account, develop a cadre of NGO professionals with skills in rural marketing and facilitate capacity, building of NGO's for organising micro credit related activities. Proper training and counselling in the direction of equipping the existing entrepreneurs with skills to encourage planned growth, can really bring about a visible change in the performance graph of small scale enterprises. Realising this necessity EDI organises performance improvement programmes, Growth programmes, Intrapreneurship programmes, Export and strategic programmes, small industry management Assistant programmes and programmes on succession planning for Entrepre-neurial continuity aiming at imbibing advanced functional management and strategic techniques for surviving and growing in a state of rapid environmental, technological and organisational flux.

With the objective of strengthening entrepreneurship development institutes and entrepreneurship development programmes the institute designed its programmes focussing on capacity building of EDIs through foundation and functional trainers training programmes, skill development programmes to help trainer motivators organise growth programmes for existing entrepreneurs and developing first generation entrepreneurs through Open Learning Programme in Entreprenuership. The support system plays a crucial role in the survival and growth of potential and existing entrepreneurs. The constituents of support system are officials of development organisations, financial institutions and administrative/monitoring departments. EDI organises conferences, workshops, seminars for interaction between NGO's and bankers to facilitate creation and development of business enterprise. The institute has taken several research initiatives in the area of industrial environment, industrial clusters policy and support system and has designed programmes to sensitise the environment to provide extensive support to potential existing entrepreneurs, encourage waven entrepreneurs to come forward, develop linkage among all those who work to support and promote entrepreneurship and inculcate intrapreneurial skills to help government officials play a proactive role.

Besides the above varied programmes the institute has an innovative centre sponsored by National Science and Technology Entrepreneurship Development Board and is expected to play a facilitatory role in bringing ideas from laboratories to the industrial area and encourage evolution of technology driven entrepreneurs by making available to them information on new and advanced technologies.

EDI has a separate Centre for Research and Entrepreneurship Education and Development (CREED) with the responsibility of serving as a bridge between academics and training consultancy in the field of entrepreneurship.

The institute has effectively supported entrepreneurship development activities throughout the globe at the behest of international developmental agencies such as UNIDO, ILO, SARC, World Bank, Commonwealth secretariat and governments of developing countries. EDIs expertise in entrepreneurship development, New entrepreneurs creation, business opportunity identification and project appraisal techniques are globally appreciated. In recognition of the international statute the United Nations Economic and Social Commission of Asia and Pacific (ESCAP) Bangkok, Thailand has declared EDI as Centre of Excellence. Inter-regional Centre (IRC) for Entrepreneurship and Investment Training sponsored by UNIDO and Government of India is another feather in its cap.

### National Institute for Entrepreneurship and Small Business Development (NIESBUD)

NIESBUD was established as an apex body to co-ordinate the activities of various institutes and agencies engaged in Entrepreneurship development to organise and conduct training programmes for them. The institute is registered as a society under Government of India Societies Act, XXI of 1860 and started functioning from 6th July, 1983. It is also the secretariat of the National Entrepreneurship development board the apex body which determines policy for entrepreneurship in the country. The institute provides training to various target groups by evolving standardised model syllabi for the respective groups. The programmes organised by the institute are government funded and its training activities are restricted to stimulating, supporting and sustaining entrepreneurship, in areas where the demand for such programmes is high or where there are no organisations conducting such programmes.

NIESBUD plays a supportive role in developing the efficiency of organisations which are directly or indirectly engaged in promoting entrepreneurship. The main objectives of the institute are to accelerate the process of entrepreneurship development and to support and help institutes/agencies involved in entrepreneurship development to improve their efficiency. The other objectives are to evolve standard processes of selection, training, support and sustenance to potential entrepreneurs, to provide vital information and to provide functional forums, for interaction and exchange of experiences helpful for policy formulation and modification at various levels. The policy direction and guidance to the institute is provided by its governing council whose chairman and vice-chairman are the Union Industry Minister and Union State Minister of Industry respectively.

,The institute has organised programmes to various target groups including entrepreneurs, officials from support and service agencies, organisations, professions, and promoters of entrepreneurship from government, non-government and voluntary organisatios. The programmes of the institute consist of Trainers Training programmes, Trainers/promoters orientation programme; small business promoters programme, small enterprise continuing education programme, Entrepreneurship orientation programme for Heads of Departments and Senior executives. Some of the groups benefitted by NIESBUD training are progressors/researchers from academic institutions like IIT, Engineering colleges, Senior officers from commercial banks, TCOs, SIDO officers, officers of Shramik Vidyapeeths, etc.

The programmes initiated and sponsored by NIESBUD are constantly evaluated and revised to suit the changing needs in the area of entrepreneurship and small Business Development. The institute is engaged in creating a climate conducive to the emergence of entrepreneurship and in developing favourable attitude amongst the general public in support of those who opt for entrepreneurial career.

**Small Industries Development Bank of India (SIDBI)**

SIDBI was established in April 1990 under an act of the Indian Parliament as wholly owned Subsidiary of Industrial Development Bank of India (IDBI). The main objectives of SIDBI are to serve as the principal financial institution for promotion, financing and development of Industry in the small scale sector and co-ordinating the functions of other institutions engaged in similar activities. The Bank, right from its inception has strived to make effective use of the existing network of institutions serving the small scale sector. Further the bank has collaborated with various national and international development organisations to synergise the efforts in serving the small scale sector. The network of SIDBI consists of 5 regional offices and 43 branches with its head office at Lucknow. It extends reliance assistance through 888 primary lending institutions such as commerical banks, SFCs which in turn have over 60,000 branches throughout India.

SIDBI was ranked 21st in terms of assets, 34th in terms of capital among the 50 development banks of the world by 'The Banker', London in its May 1997 issue. The schemes of assistance of SIDBI for the small scale sector is through three routes.

- Indirect assistance, namely, refinance and bills rediscounting is channelised by SIDBI through a network of 888 primary lending institutions including banks and state financial corporations which have over 65,000 outlets.
- Direct assistance is through its own network of 38 offices (5 regional and 33 branch offices) in India.
- Development and support services of SIDBI are focussed at enterprise promotion with emphasis on rural industrialisation, Human Resource development of small scale industry sector, technology upgradation, special emphasis programmes like quality and environment management and information dissemination.

The programmes for enterprise promotion include micro-credit schemes, rural industries programmes, Mahila Vikas Nidhi and entrepreneur development programmes. Programmes for HRD of SSIs are Small Industries Management Assistant Programme (SIMPA) and Skill-cum Technology Upgradation Programmes (STUP). Quality and environment and management programmes and workshops on quality management technology and assistance to create awareness among the SSIs for abatement of environmental pollution and information dissemination aims at promoting new units by identification and publicity of viable project ideas and business opportunities through publication of project profiles, broadcasting, Udyog Sadhana-radio programmes and production of video films on various entrepreneurship themes and telecasting them through electronic media. SIDBI also co-ordinates its efforts with the Non-government organisations (NGOs), marketing and training institutions, research organisations, etc., for effective reach.

**Small Industries Development Organisation (SIDO)**

Pioneering the institutional infrastructure for the development of small scale industries at the central level is Small Industries Development Organisation at New Delhi with a large number of field outfits and subordinate formations providing a wide ranging techno-economic consultancy services and support. SIDO is headed by the Development commissioners, Small Scale Industries and is an attached office of the department of Small Scale Industry, Agro and Rural Industries, Ministry of Industry, Government of India. It is an apex body and a nodal agency for formulating, co-ordinating and monitoring policies and programmes for promotion and development of small scale industries. SIDO renders comprehensive services including consultancy in techno-economic and managerial aspects, training common facility services, testing and tooling facilities, marketing assistance, etc., for small scale units. These services are provided through a network of field agencies and institutions created for the purpose. Important among them are Small Industries Service Institutes and Branch Small Industry Service Institutes, Regional Testing Centres and Field Testing Stations, Tool Rooms and Tool Design Institutes and Process-cum Product Development Centres.

SISIs are 28 in number and branch SISIs 30—which are set up in state capitals and other places all over the country. The important functions of these institutes constitute conducting EDPs and promotional programmes, providing technical support and consultancy services to entrepreneurs and conducting state industrial and district industrial potential surveys. There are four regional testing centres and ten field testing stations providing testing and consultancy facilities and conducting training programmes. The tool rooms and tool design institutes assist in tool design, manufacture of tools, figs, fixtures, etc., provide training facilities to tool makers and offers consultancy.

The product-cum-process development centres serve as Research and Development Institutions in areas of dense industry clusters. They aid in product design and innovation, product and process improvement and development of improved packaging technology, man power development and training, etc. Apart from the above field agencies there are other associated specialised institutions like National Small Industries Corporation (NSIC), New Delhi providing machinery for small scale industries on hire purchase basis, marketing support, technology assistance, equipment leasing, etc. National Institute for Entrepreneurship and Small Business Development, New Delhi and National Institute of Small Industry Extention Training, Hyderabad for entrepreneurship development and training and SIDBI for financing SSI projects coordination between central and state/union territory governments is effected by SSIs Board which is an apex advisory body constituted to render advice to the government on all issues pertaining to small scale sector.

In addition there are a large number of organisations and institutions in States/Union Terrritories to provide various specialised inputs and services like the DICs, Small Industry Development Corporations, State Small Scale Industries Development Corporations, commissioners and directing of industries, etc. Apart from organising entrepreneurial development and training programmes and offering technical and testing assistance, SIDO also organises awareness and motivational programmes to educate and train the small scale industries in the matter of pollution abatement and Energy conservation programmes keeping in view the high cost of energy and high levels of energy consumption in some of the specific industrial sectors, namely, foundry, forging, rerolling, glass/ceramic/porcelain industries, plywood industries, etc. In addition Awareness and Educational programmes on total quality management and ISO-9000 are organised and SSIs are given financial support by way of reimbursement of 75 per cent of their expenses for obtaining ISO-9000 certification subject to a maximum of 75,000 rupees.

### National Alliance of Young Entrepreneurs (NAYE)

NAYE is a national organisation of young entrepreneurs of the country. It has been a pioneer in promotion and development of Entrepreneurship among women. In the internationally acknowledged women's year 1975 NAYE had set up a women's wing to take special care of the interests of women entrepreneurs and one of its major achievements in creating and nurturing a new class of women entrepreneurs and enabling them to acquire their rightful place in the Indian Economy. NAYE convened a conference of women entrepreneurs in November 1975 at New Delhi to discuss at length the steps to be taken to make women self-reliant and to raise their status in the society. Since then three international conferences on better access to capital, infrastructure and markets; eight national conventions of women entrepreneurs have been organised in different cities of our country.

The waver's wing of NAYE assists women entrepreneurs in getting management and production capabilities, identifying investment opportunities and in sponsoring delegations, participation in trade fairs, exhibitions, etc. NAYE attends to the problems of women entrepreneurs by taking up individual cases with appropriate authorities and it also performs the function of organising seminars, workshops and training programmes for giving the women entrepreneurs wider exposure to the available facilities. In addition NAYE's women wing performs the function of lobbying for women entrepreneurs in press, parliament, state legislatures and other forums and advocates effectively for giving women entrepreneurs a rightful place in the Indian Economy.

The Association of Women Industrialists/Entrepreneurs of Maharashtra was set up in May 1985 and has 400 members all over the state. Its head office is at Pune and branches at Mumbai, Aurangabad, Nasik, and Dhulia. WIMA is a part of NAYE and its main objective is to provide a forum for members to help them sell their products. It also conducts training programmes for women entrepreneurs.

### State Bank of India (SBI)

SBI is the only bank amongst the commerical banks in India,

which has evolved a comprehensive programme for entrepreneurship development. From the traditional role of commerical banks, SBI pioneered as a premier banking institution by asuming the role of a development bank. It has formulated an elaborate plan to conduct entrepreneurship development programmes, particularly in the backward areas and started conducting EDPs since 1978. As per the bank's model, the EDPs consist of one month intensive training in behavioural sciences, management aspects and field training and during this period the entire cost of boarding and lodging is borne by the bank. The EDPs consists of three phases:

*(i)* the initiation phase aimed at identifying persons with potential for development and entrepreneurial disposition,

*(ii)* the development phase to impart training programmes in developing motivation and management skills, and

*(iii)* the support phase to encourage and support entrepreneurs to establish and operate the enterprise effectively.

The Bank recognised the importance of small scale industries in Industrial development and started financing SSIs on a large scale. A package of schemes and programmes was formulated by the bank to cater to the specific needs of the small scale sector. The schemes are— *(i) the liberalised scheme* of financing SSIs wherein 75 per cent of the project cost is met as bank loan; *(ii) entrepreneurs scheme* for financing technically qualified persons whereunder the entire project cost could be financed by way of term loan, and *(iii) equity fund scheme* for providing interest free loan to meet the equity gap up to Rs.1 lakh.

**National Small Industries Corporation (NSIC)**

NSIC is a government undertaking, set up in 1955 with the objective of providing machinery and equipment to small enterprises on hire purchase basis and assisting them in procuring government orders for various items of stores. Formerly the corporation had four subsidiary corporations at Delhi, Mumbai, Calcutta and Madras. However, since 1961 all the subsidiary corporations have been amalgamated with the main corporation and three branch offices have been set up at Mumbai, Calcutta and Chennai. The Delhi subsidary corporation has been merged with the parent corporation and its work is looked after by a separate Delhi Cell set up in it.

The main functions of the corporation include providing machinery on hire purchase basis to SSIs, to distribute basic raw materials through their raw materials depots, to import and distribute components and parts to actual small scale users in specific industries and to arrange for the marketing of products of SSIs by starting emporia and sales depots and promote their exports. In addition, NSIC assists small enterprises to participate in the store purchase programme of the central government and construct industrial estates and establish production-cum-training centres for the entrepreneurs. NSIC has opened its offices in some of the states to improve the development efforts and to supplement the activities of state small Industries corporations and District Industry Services Institutes.

**National Institute of Small Industry Extention Training (NISIET)**

NISIET was established as a Central Training Institute (CTI) in 1960. It aims at providing training initially for officers of SIDO. Later the activities were expanded and was renamed as SIET and later declared as NISIET.

The major activity of the institute is to provide entrepreneurial training and to meet the varied requirements of entrepreneurs. A number of new programmes were planned which covered almost all aspects such as development, management documentation and behavioural aspects. North East regional centre of NISIET was set up at Guwahati during 1979 as to develop that region. Major part of training takes place at the institute which has facilities like well-equipped seminar rooms, Audio-visual section for providing training, a documentation centre and a hostel attached to train 160 participants at a time. The institute organised training programmes for other developing countries of Afro-Asia, the Pacific and the Caribbean regions. The institute organised and conducted ten international programmes of duration of 88 weeks in which 183 officers from 32 countries participated. The centre has been organising a series of EDPs which are jointly sponsored by NEC, IDBI, IFCI, ICICI and department of Industries of the respective state governments of the region.

## Directorates of Industries of the State Government and State Small Industries Corporations

The work relating to the development of industries in general and small scale industries in particular is looked after by the Directorates of Industries in each state and Union Territory. There are 22 such directorates all over the country. Each organisation is staffed with administrative and technical officers at the state headquarters and by District Industries officer with appropriate support staff in each district. The state directorates run various training schemes, production schemes and common facilities schemes. They also provide facilities of developed industrial land and build up factory sheds in industrial estates, allocate quotas of scarce raw materials, certify import requirements and organise industrial co-operatives. Their functions are varied and have grown with the development and diversification of small industry sector. The general assistance of these directorates include organising EDPs, providing industrial accomodation, raw materials, machinery on hire-purchase, etc. It activities under marketing assistance involve export assistance, price preference, quality marking, etc. These directorates provide financial assistance in the forms of loans, subsidies, margin money loans, rebates on handicrafts, raw material units, etc. State Small Industries Corporations have been set up by 13 state governments as private limited bodies to undertake a number of commercial activities. The most important of these are distribution of scarce raw materials, supply of machinery on hire purchase, construction and management of industrial estates, procurement of orders from government depots to be sub-contracted to small industries, assistance in export marketing and in certain circumstances provision of finance, technology and managerial assistance to small enterprises.

## Khadi and Village Industries Commission (KVIC)

KVIC is a statutory organisation established in 1957 by an act of the parliament and is engaged in promoting khadi and village industries with a view of creating employment opportunities in the rural areas thereby strengthening the rural economy. It is an autonomous body which took over from its predecessor the "All India Khadi and Village Industries Board" set up in 1953. KVIC has 27 state board, 148 registered institutions and over 29,955 industrial co-operatives. KVIC has around 11,000 sales outlets in the country.

The commission functions with the social objective of providing employment, economic objective of producing suitable saleable articles and the wider objective of creating self reliance amongst the people and building up a strong rural community spirit.

The functions of KVIC are to plan, organise and implement programmes for the promotion and development of Khadi and village industries. The main functions include training of persons engaged in production of Khadi and village industries, building reserves of raw materials and supplying them to khadi and village industries, to provide for sale and marketing of the products and to encourage research in the techniques of production of khadi and village products. In addition the commission encourages development of khadi and village industries and ensures genuineness of their products.

KVIC is a unique national organisation in the country which has its roots in the villages as its activities cover 1.5 lakhs villages in the country. Around 26 per cent of its beneficiaries belong to the scheduled castes and scheduled tribes and inhabitants in the hilly and border area. The women beneficiaries are also high constituting around 45 per cent.

**State Financial Corporations (SFCs)**

State financial corporations have been set in various states with the main objective of extending assistance to industrial units in tiny, small scale and medium scale sectors and service enterprises. These corporations have been playing a significant role in taking the states to their rightful place on the industrial map of the country. Andhra Pradesh State Financial Corporation (APSFC) was formed in 1956 and is offering liberal financial assistance for acquiring fixed assets like land, building and machinery. The term loan asssistance from the corporation is available in the range of Rs. 10,000 to Rs. 150 lakhs per unit and is offered through various convenient and easily payable schemes to suit individual requirements.

APSFC has provided finance to thousands of units during

the past 4 decades. With its widespread network of 5 zonal offices at Vijayawada, Warrangal, Tirupati, Vishakhapatnam and Hyderabad, 2 field offices at Hindupur (Anantpur District) and Chittoor (Chittoor district) and 25 branch offices in reaching the farthest corners of the state to provide door step assistance to the entrepreneurs facilitating accelaration and balanced industrial development. The branch offices have a sanctioning power up to Rs. 10 lakhs, Zonal offices from 10-20 lakhs and Head office from 20 lakhs to 150 lakhs.

Industrial concerns under any form of ownership, whether it be a proprietory or partnership concern, Joint Hindu family, registered co-operative society, private or public limited are eligible for financial assistance.

Any industrial concern with a project cost not exceeding Rs. 5 crores is eligible for financial assistance and wherever necessary APSFC undertakes joint financing with other financial institutions, state/central commercial banks like APIDC, IFCI, ICICI, IDBI, etc.

The schemes for financial assistance of APSFC include equipment refinance scheme, modernisation scheme, Scheme for Hotels, Motels, Restaurants, schemes for tourism related facilities, assistance to hospitals and nursing homes and for acquiring electro-medical equipment, transport loan scheme for acquiring road laying equipment and heavy earth moving equipment, single window scheme, XO category scheme and many more.

The special schemes of the corporation include Mahila Udyam Nidhi scheme for women entrepreneurs, National Equity Fund scheme for existing tiny, SSIs and service enterprises undertaking expansion, modernisation and SEMFEX scheme for ex-servicemen, disabled service personnel and widows of ex-servicemen. The rate of interest and the loan eligibility varies with the type of scheme of assistance.

### District Industries Centres (DICs)

The DIC programme was started on 1 May 1978 as a central sponsored scheme during the seventh plan period with the government of India sharing its expenditure with the State governments on 50-50 basis. DICs have been established in almost all districts of the country and the total number of approved DICs are 422 covering 431 districts. The main objective of the DIC Programme is to develop and promote small, tiny, cottage sector industries in the country and to generate employment opportunities especially among the rural and backward areas of the country. The DICs are envisaged as a single window interacting agency with the entrepreneur. At the district level, services and support to small entrepreneurs are provided under the single roof through the district Industry centres. Registration of small industries is done at the respective district industry centre. DICs play an important role in providing assistance to entrepreneurs at the pre-investment and post-investment stages, in setting up industries, particularly in rural and backward areas of the country.

Prime Minister Rojgar Yojana (PMRY) for providing self employment to educated unemployed youth is also implemented by the DICs. This scheme was announced in August 1993 and was launched on 2 October 1993 to provide self-employment opportunities to 10 lakhs educated unemployed youth by setting up 7 lakh micro-enterprises. This scheme has associated reputed Non-government organisations in implementation, especially in the selection, training of entrepreneurs and preparation of project profiles.

The development of Entrepreneurship depends very much on organisation, education, stimulation and motivation of the clientele through a concerted and systematic approach focussing on individual and groups. The government developmental agencies and institutions have made serious attempts to undertake the task of entrepreneurial promotion. Most of the promotional activities are directed towards the financial and physical facilities with a strong belief that there will be an automatic flow of entrepreneurs if such facilities are created especially in the backward states of India. Apart from the financial and physical inputs, entrepreneurial skills are being given due importance. Entrepreneur Development Programmes (EDPs) have become a novel approach for harnessing the vast untapped human talent and are of the most talked social development activities. The success of these EDPs depends on proper participant selection, proper training, making suitable organisational arrangement for disseminating information, putting efforts to impart more technical and practical training and providing full assistance not only in preparation of project reports but also in meeting their financial requirements. The various financial/technical institutions and organisations and the different departments of the central and state governments engaged in entrepreneurship development should establish a greater degree of co-operation, liaison, closer working relationships and better understanding. No tangible results can, therefore, be expected unless all the agencies involved in the task of entrepreneurship development work with determination, zeal and a sense of dedication and commitment.

# 7

# Entrepreneurial Management

—*Prof. K. Seshaiah*
—*Dr. M. Munirami Reddy*

**Introduction**

There is a total confusion in the minds of theoriticians and practitioners alike with regard to entrepreneurship and management, especially in business organisations. This has led to ambiguity in the role perceptions of managers as to what are the managerial tasks and entrepreneurial tasks in an organisation. As a result it has become a difficult job for the trainers in imparting the requisite knowledge, skills and techniques to the trainees for enabling them to play a balanced role of 'being' a manager and 'becoming' a entrepreneur. Absence of this is obvious in growth stunted organisations with all round stagnation. The clarity in this repect would make, specially the Indian organisations, to meet the new challenges and changes in the wake of liberalisation, globalisation and international competitiveness in all sectors and forms of organisations. The purpose of this paper is to explain the entrepreneurial management theory as applicable to both the existing and new business enterprises.

**Meaning and Scope of Entrepreneurship**

Many a definition has been advanced on entrepreneur and entrepreneurship since J.B. Say's definition of entrepreneur who "shifts economic resources out of the areas of lower and into an area of higher productivity and greater yield". The limitation in this definition is that it does not tell who performs this function. Popular conception of entrepreneur is one who starts his own, new and small business, but every new small business need not stand for entrepreneurship. Besides being new and small, a business unit has certain special characteristics. Entrepreneurs of the businesses creates something new, something different, changing value. Another misconception to be dispelled is that to be entrepreneurial, enterprise business unit need not be small and new. Enterpreneurship may be practised by big and old business units alike. Further entrepreneurship is not confined to economic institutions. It extends to all institutions, economic and social and to ownership patterns—private—public and co-operative sector enterprises. Further to be an entrepreneur one need not be owner, capital, or investor. The present development banks, which mobilise other people's money for allocation to the areas of higher productivity and yield, are entrepreneurs, though not owners. Entrepreneur is also not employer but can be an employee or someone who works alone, i.e., self-employed.

After defining entrepreneur negatively, it is but appropriate to focus on what is entrepreneurship. "Everyone who can face up to decision making can learn to be an entrepreneur and to behave entrepreneurially. Entrepreneurship, then, is behaviour rather than personality trait." Foundation of entrepreneurship lies in concept and theory. This theory is theory of economy and soceity which sees change as normal and indeed as healthy. This economic and social theory sees the major task in society as doing something different rather than doing better what is already being done. In Schumpeter's words "entrepreneurial task is 'creative destruction'." Hence entrepreneur always searches for change, responds to it and exploits it as an opportunity.

Though risk is associated with entrepreneurship it is not enormous. Even if the entrepreneurs are moderately successful, the rewards more than offset whatever the risks there might be. Entrepreneur innovates so innovation is the specific instrument of entrepreneurship. Through this act he creates resources in the sense that he finds economic value for something in nature. Innovation, therefore, is economic or social rather than technical. Sources of innovation may be internal as well as external to the enterprise or industry.

## Innovation as Instrument of Entrepreneurship

There are principles of innovation that constitute the core of discipline of innovation, which can be formulated and presented in do's and don'ts form.

### *Do's*

*(i)* Scientific innovation starts with analysis of innovative opportunities. It is of limited use being aware of opportunities only; but the search should be systematised. Entrepreneurs should look at figures for innovation. Hence innovation is conceptual.

*(ii)* Innovation is perceptual too. They look at people for innovation. As an imperative innovation demands going out to look, to speak and listen to customers or users. Innovators use both their left and right minds. They use both their conceptual and perceptual skills.

*(iii)* Effective innovation should be simple, i.e., doing only one thing at a time and be specific focussing attention on need it satisfies and result that it produces.

*(iv)* Effective innovation starts small. It is derivative of (ii) and (iii) above. Innovation should try to do one specific thing. Start near to go far.

### *Don'ts*

*(i)* Innovators should not try to be clever. To facilitate handling of innovations by ordinary people, and so as to gain size and importance as well, innovations should be simple in design and execution.

*(ii)* Innovations should not diversify or splinter. They require concentrated energy unified effort behind them.

*(iii)* Innovations should not be for future. Innovations should be for present.

### *Three Conditions*

Apart from do's and don'ts three sufficient conditions can be stipulated for effective innovation:

*(i)* Innovation is work. Effective innovation requires knowledge which is necessary but not a sufficient condition. It requires hard, focussed and purposeful work.

*(ii)* To succeed, innovations should be built on innovators strength. Innovators should be temperamentally attuned to innovative opportunity which also should match their knowledge and performance capacity.

*(iii)* Innovations are an effect in economy and society.

They bring change in the behaviour of the people or processes, i.e., in how people work and produce something.

**Entrepreneurial Management in Existing Business**

Principles of entrepreneurship are same whether entrepreneur is existing large business unit, newly set-up venture, single handed or public service institution. These principles are collectively termed as entrepreneurial management.

**Entrepreneurial Management Policies in Existing Business**

In existing business the entrepreneurial management must make its manager greedy for new things. For this to happen, there should be specific policies.

*(i)* Innovation, rather than holding on to already existing, should be made attractive or beneficial. Managers must be made to understand that it preserves and perpetuates the organisation, and serves as a foundation to job security and job success. There must be systematic abandonment of outworn, obsolete and unproductive policies. Innovation requires major effort. So existing business must be able to free best performers for the challenges of innovation.

*(ii)* The fact the product, service, process, technologies, markets, etc., usually have short life expectancies must be recognised. Their analysis of life cycle should lead to diagnosis which in turn leads to judgement which demands experience besides analysis.

*(iii)* This analysis provides information which is essential to define, a given business, how much of innovation is needed, in what area and in what time frame.

*(iv)* After analysis of the existing business and ascertaining the innovation gap and need, what needs to be done is formulation of entrepreneurial plans with objectives for innovation and time deadlines.

### *Entrepreneurial Management Practices in Existing Business*

Requirements of entrepreneurship in existing business are the following practices:

*(i)* Focus should be on opportunity. People see what is presented to them. In most of the cases what is presented are problems. confining only to problems, opportunities die of neglect. Therefore, opportunities should also be attended to.

*(ii)* Entrepreneurial companies always look for people and unit that do better and differently. They ask them to explain underlying causes of success.

*(iii)* These companies have also informal meetings of top management with the junior people to hear from them innovative business opportunities.

### *Innovative Performance Measurement in Existing Business*

Innovative performance must be included among the measures by which business is controlled. Feedback from results to expectations must be built into innovative project, which indicates quality and reliability of innovative plans and efforts. Next, a systematic review of all innovative efforts of the business should be developed. Finally, comparison should be attempted between innovative performance and innovative objectives, market standing and its performance as a business as a whole.

### *Innovative Structures in Existing Business*

Policies, practices and measurements do remove impediments to innovation. Ultimately it is the people who innovate and they work in structures. Hence there is a need to create structure in which people becomes innovative. This entails the following. The entrepreneurial venture has to be organised from the present and existing. New ventures should be assigned to someone in top management, to have focus on it. No venture should be set up separately as it can be asked to bear the burdens until it matures to shoulder them. Returns on new ventures should be measured separately from the existing business. A person or competent group should be held clearly accountable for new venture in the existing buisness.

### *Staffing in the Existing Business*

What is needed of the people working in entrepreneurial

organisation is willingness to work hard and persistently, willingness to exercise self-discipline, willingness to adapt and apply right policies and procedures.

### *Don'ts of Entrepreneurial Management of Existing Business*

The first and foremost is that entrepreneurial units should not be mixed with existing ones. Whatever may be the benefits of diversification, it does not mix up with innovation and entrepreneurship. Any innovation that takes existing business away from its field is rarely successful. It is not fruitful to make business entrepreneurial by acquiring small entrepreneurial ventures.

### *Entrepreneurial Management is New Venture*

Whereas in the existing business the controlling word in the entrepreneurial management is "entrepreneurial", in the new ventures it is "management".

### *Requirements of Entrepreneurial Management in New Ventures*

Unless new venture develops into a new business, i.e., a viable, operating and organised present, and makes sure of being managed, it will not survive.

*(i) The Need for Market Focus*

The new venture should start out with the assumption that its product or service may find customers in markets. To be market driven also requires that the new venture should be willing to experiment. This is the problem of infant new ventures.

*(ii) Financial Foresight*

In the next stage of growth of new ventures, the problem is the lack of adequate financial focus and of the right financial policies. Focus should be on cash flow, capital and control, not profits, But this order is reversed in most of the cases.

*(iii) Building a Top Management Team*

Lack of top management is one of the causes of failure when the new venture is about to be on the threshold of becoming a successful, established and going concern. When the venture has outgrown being managed by one or two persons, the new venture top management team at the top. The founder has to learn to become the leader of a team.

*(iv) Contribution of the Founders of New Ventures*

As new venture develops and grows, the role and relationships of the founders invariably change. If this is not accepted, they stunt the business and even destroy it. For the new, growing ventures, independent and objective outside advice is needed.

## Mega Economic Environment for Entrepreneurial Management

Entrepreneurial society requires innovations in two important areas.

*(i) Policy to Take Care of Redundant Workers*

The problem of redundant workers is soluble if an economy becomes entrepreneurial. Though Entrepreneurial economy creates new jobs, there should be organised effort to train the surplus workers and to place them in new jobs, since they cannot do it for themselves.

*(ii) Abandonment of Worn Out Social Policies and Obsolete Public Service Institutions*

Government policies and agencies are after all human, not divine, which get obsolete fairly soon, unless they are re-enacted. The laws have not worked, partly because objective criteria as to when a agency becomes dysfunctional or lacking. There is no organised process of abandonment. Secondly, no alternative method is developed for achieving what an ineffectual or government agency was originally supposed to achieve.

## Need for Competitive Macro Policy in India for Entrepreneurial Management of Its Business

Competitive policy is a set-up of government measures that directly impact on individual enterprise behaviour and on the structure of industries. The objective of this policy is to foster economic efficiency, economic growth, and international competitiveness. India, for long, suffered from lack of a macro competition policy due to highly regulated business environment, potential losses resulting from restrictive government policies, assured protected markets, guaranteeing markets irrespective of efficiency, subsidisation of losses through budget support in the case of public enterprises, etc. In the New Economic Policy, 1991, changes were aimed at creating a far more open and competitive environment in India.

## Conclusion

Economic philosophies governing the world economic systems shifted from *laissez faire* and welfarism to present entrepreneurial economies. A few of all the enterprises, be it business or non-business, are really entrepreneurial. Entrepreneurship is economic and social theory which recognises change as a norm and as healthy. Innovation is an instrument of entrepreneurship. Entrepreneur searches for change, responds to it and exploits it. Principles of entrepreneurship form the core of discipline called entrepreneurial management which applies to existing business, new ventures and public service institutions. Since the conditions and problems these institutions face may be different, the policies, practices, measurement systems, structures, staffing also vary between them. New Economic Policies, 1991, in India were aimed at creating macro economic competitive policy to increase the efficiency of the business units abandoning or revising statutes and policies and public service institutions which had become obsolete.

## References

1. Peter, F. Drucker, *Innovation and Entrepreneurship: Practice and Principles*, Affiliated East-West Press Private Limited, New Delhi, 1991.
2. *Ibid.*, pp. 134-40
3. *Ibid.*, pp.151-74
4. S.L. Rao, "Towards a National Competitive Policy for India", *Economic and Politicial Weekly*, Vol. XXXIII , No. 9, pp. 4-31.

# 8

# Impact of Entrepreneurship on Economic Growth in Pondicherry

—*Dr. P. Palanichamy*

## Introduction

The development or under-development is the reflection of the abundance or scarcity of entrepreneurship in any society. The vital aspect for the growth of a modern society in any country is the adequate and increasing supply of enterprise. Development does not occur spontaneously as a natural consequence, when economic conditions are in some sense 'right', a catalyst or agent is need and this requires entrepreneurial activity.

Entrepreneurship comprises all those productive functions that are not thought to be rewarded by wages, rent, or interest. It is not associated with routine human efforts (labour). It does not involve the use of indestructable natural resources, i.e., land, it does not imply the provision of capital funds. In other words entrepreneurship meant the function of seeking investment and production opportunity, organising an enterprise to undertake a new production process, raising capital, hiring labour, arranging the supply of raw materials, finding site, introducing a new technique and commodities, discovering new sources of raw materials and selection of top managers for day-to-day operations of the enterprise.

Entrepreneurship in brief calls for "enterprise" which is defined as an undertaking, task or adventure of a bold or different nature and also as the ability to think and start new schemes.

**Definition and Meaning of Entrepreneur**

*Peter F. Drucker* defines entrepreneur "as one who always searches for changes, responds to it, and exploits it as an opportunity."

*Schumpter* emphasis "innovation as an essential quality of an entrepreneur."

*Walker* describes him "as a person endowed with more than average mans capacities in the task of organising and co-ordinating the various other factors of production."

According to *William Diamond*, "Entrepreneurship is equivalent to 'enterprise' which involves the willingness to assume risk in undertaking an economic activity, particularly a new one. It may involve an innovation but not necessarily so. It always involves risk taking, decision making, although neither risk nor decision making may be of great significance. Thus, entrepreneurship refers to the qualities which are required to innovate, start a new enterprise, accept the challenge and bear the risk."

**Entrepreneurship and Economic Development**

The most vital aspect for the growth of a modern society in any country is an adequate and increasing supply of enterprises. It has emerged as the most important factor of production for three reasons. Firstly, whatever may be the supply of other factors, nothing happens until such factors of production are galvanised into action by enterprise. Secondly, an adequate supply of enterprise can, to a considerable extent, make up for shortages of others. Thirdly, enterprise is an intangible factor and the rise and fall of the nations bear testimony to the intangible factors such as initiative, imagination and determination of the people of these countries.

In the entrepreneurship development of any country/state, the institutions involved in are the:

(*a*) District Industries Centre.
(*b*) Productivity Council.
(*c*) Small Industries Services Institutes.
(*d*) Lead Banks of the State/District collaboration with EDI(I)

and the institution involved in providing financial and other assistance.

(*e*) All India and State level financial corporations.

(*f*) Commercial Banks.

(*g*) National Small Industries Corporation (NSIC).

(*h*) Small Industries development Bank of India (SIDBI).

**Scope and Objectives of this Paper**

This small piece of work aims at:

1. tracing the steps taken by the Government of Pondicherry, and its agencies in the promotion of entrepreneurship, its consequent growth of Industries and the economy.
2. it also attempts to measure the growth in the EDPs.
3. to measure the relationship between the EDPs and Economic growth, and
4. finally it attempts to find out the impact of entrepreneurship on productivity.

The methodology adopted for this study is the collection of primary data as to the number of EDPs conducted by various agencies through interviews and discussions.

The statistical tools used for this study are simple tools like regression equation, multiple regression and percentage, etc.

The French Government used it only as its trading centre and hence there was no Directorate of Industries and Commerce here, but, it was only after its annexation to the Union of India it was set up. Apart from this, the SISI and NSIC were also set up by the Government of India. The Government of Pondicherry on its part also set up the Pondicherry Industrial Promotion Development and Investment Corporation (PIPDIC), the State Financial Corporation, Pondicherry Productivity Council; and a few industrial estates.

The entrepreneurship or the industrial progress started only after sixties or after declaring it as a industrially backward district in the year 1971 or in the eighties. That is why the data pertaining to the Entrepreneurial Development Programmes (EDP) conducted, number of industries set up consequent to this, investments made in these, goods and services produced or the employment generated are made available by the Directorate of Industries and Commerce, and the District Industries Centre only from 1984-85.

***Period of Study***

Thus the period of study became 14 years commencing from 1984-85 to 1997-98.

**Socio Economic Condition of Union Territory of Pondicherry**

Pondicherry is a centrally administered small union territory having a population of 8,07,045 and land area of 492 sq. km. While Jawaharlal Nehru was laying strong foundations for modern industrialized nation, Pondicherry joined the Union of India in the year 1954 with three large textile mills and some five odd small industrial institutions employing about 8000 people.

In the Union Territory of Pondicherry, the institutions involved in the conduct and promotion of entrepreneurships are:

1. District Industries Centre (DIC)
2. Pondicherry Productivity Council
3. Small Industries Service Institute
4. Indian Bank, the lead bank in collaboration with
5. Pondicherry Chamber of Commerce.

Institutions involved in providing financial and other assistance in Pondicherry are:

1. Pondicherry Industrial Promotion Development and Investment Corporation (PIPDIC).
2. S.B.I Small Business Branch.
3. District Industries Centre.
4. National Small Industries Corporation (NSIC)
5. Small Industries Development Bank of India (SIDBI).
6. Branches of Commercial Banks under Lead Bank Scheme.

A small discussion on the objectives and the role played by these institutions in the promotion of the entrepreneurship and economic development through entrepreneurship is imperative here.

**District Industries Centre**

This is an institution created to provide all help needed by small scale industrialists under one roof. This can also help the medium and large scale industries once they file for industrial licence. IEM with secretariat for industrial approvals with the Ministry of Industries, Government of India, for getting clearances/licences to be obtained from various local authorities. It also undertakes many management development and training programmes like inplant training and training in handicrafts and coir industry.

The Pondicherry Productivity Council even though founded in 1988 was established only in 1966. It is a premier institute in the UTI of Pondicherry in performing the role of catalyst for productivity, promotion, demonstrating innovative skills through consultancies both at the macro and enterprise levels through specialists in the frontier areas of management and technology oriented disciplines. Besides providing training and consultancy services, it undertakes systems development and other project works in the area of productivity.

SSIs are established in all the state headquarters for identifying local need/supply based industries, provide training consultancy and other support for the growth of the industries set up especially in the industrial estates. Pondicherry branch of the SISI was closed from 1997.

*Lead Bank Scheme.* Indian Bank is the Lead Bank for the UTI of Pondicherry. Because of the better per capita income the people of Pondicherry have and many people still have French Citizenship and connections, flow of money into Pondicherry is also considerable and also for other reasons, this region has large number of banks and their branches.

**Pondicherry Chamber of Commerce**

At the National level and State level, chambers of commerce are interacting with the respective governments for serving better the commerce fraternity, this also is actively involved in getting concession for the trade, commerce and industry.

*Pondicherry Industrial Promotion Development and Investment Corporation (PIPDIC):* It is a state financial corporation in this region. It was established in the year 1974. It is expected to act as industrial promotional, development and also investment corporation. It is rendering a yeoman service for promotion of small and medium scale enterprises. Term loans are sanctioned by PIPDIC under IDBI/SIDBI refinance scheme. The Union Territory of Pondicherry is also served by branches of SIDBI/NABARD here.

*SBI* has set up a separate branch for catering to the financial needs of small businesses.

*NSIC* has a branch office here which by purchasing the goods from one and selling the same to others, is able to act as a source of supply of raw materials for the buyer organisations and means to selling the goods for the seller organisations. It buys machinery and distributes the same to the industries on hire purchase also.

*THE SIDBI* is the apex bank for small scale industries. By setting up a branch of it here, it is able to serve to the SSI units of Pondicherry.

The facilitating factors for the industrial growth in the Union Territory of Pondicherry are:

*(a)* the declaring of it as industrially backward district in the year 1971, and thereby
*(b)* offering of the incentives and subsidies both by the Government of India and the Government of Pondicherry
*(c)* financial assistance provided by PIPDIC, SIDBI, Commerical Banks,
*(d)* training programmes conducted by DIC and PPC, etc.

The incentives and subsidies offered are:

1. Exemption from collection of both Central Sales Tax (CST) and Pondicherry General Sales Tax (PGST) for sale of finished products.
2. Income Tax holiday for initially five years and continued thereafter also.
3. Interest subsidy for quality products.
4. Price preference, exemption from payment of EMD and security deposit.
5. Availablity of power at lesser rates.
6. Investment subsidy offered for SC/ST entrepreneurs.
7. Incentives for pollution control equipments/energy saving devices.
8. Allotment of plots/work sheds in developed industrial estates.

Because of the Entrepreneurship development programmes, the infrastructural facilities, financial and other assistance provided, the industrial position of Pondicherry, which was having only 3 large scale textile mills and some five odd small industries, has grown to the following position as shown in Table 8.1.

**Table 8.1**
**Progress of Industries in Pondicherry**

| *Pondicherry as Part of France Employment* | *LSI* | *MSI* | *SSI* | *Total* | *Employ-ment* |
|---|---|---|---|---|---|
| *Employment* | *03* | *—* | *05* | *08* | *8000 persons* |
| Pondicherry as part of India As on 31.3.98 | 27 | 93 | 5726 | 5846 | |
| Investments (Rs. in Crores) | 578.04 | 217 | 160 | 955.04 | |
| Employment in Numbers | 14,597 | 6,305 | 46,164 | 67,066 | |
| Production | 862.17 | 668 | 1749 | 3279.17 | |

Table 8.1 shows three distinctive features:

*Firstly,* the employment generated as per Rs.100 in LSI is much less than the same in the case of SSI. The employment generating capacity of SSI is at least thrice that of the LSI.

*Secondly,* with reference to production, also, the production per Rs. 100 of investments in LSI is much lesser than the same in the SSI.

*Thirdly,* the growth of the industries in Pondicherry after its annexation to India is manifold.

For the purpose of further analysis, the trends in the growth of EDPs and consequent growth in other variables are shown in Table 8.2.

To find out the growth rate of various indicators of industries in Pondicherry, a linear regression equation was fitted between the year and other indicators. It has shown that the EDPs are growing at the rate of 9.1874 per cent per annum. Consequent to this the investments on Industries were also growing at the rate of 6.0113 per cent per annum, the productivity of these industries were growing at a rate of 5.786 per cent per annum. Because of these growth, the employment opportunities available to the people of Pondicherry or the surrounding areas were growing at the rate of 0.0844 per cent per annum. when these trends in the growth were tested with the student T.test, it revealed that except

**Table 8.2**
**Impact of Growth of EDPs on Other Factors in Pondicherry**

| *Year* | *No. of EDPs* | *No. of Benefi-ciaries* | *No. of Indust-ries Setup* | *Amount of investment made (Rs. in Lakhs)* | *Annual Production (Rs. in Crores)* | *Employ-ment Genera-ted* |
|---|---|---|---|---|---|---|
| Up to 1983-84 | 20 | 483 | 1946 | 3846.36 | 28809.10 | 18,742 |
| 1984-85 | 12 | 125 | 202 | 171.29 | 2356.11 | 1531 |
| 1985-96 | 17 | 130 | 244 | 369.86 | 8810 | 1545 |
| 1986-87 | 27 | 243 | 261 | 347.32 | 4243.30 | 1789 |
| 1987-88 | 18 | 306 | 298 | 657.64 | 3985.21 | 2297 |
| 1988-89 | 32 | 329 | 358 | 841.76 | 6199.33 | 2752 |
| 1989-90 | 21 | 331 | 277 | 78.88 | 8905.91 | 2102 |
| 1990-91 | 26 | 259 | 297 | 354.36 | 7849.57 | 2279 |
| 1991-92 | 42 | 484 | 356 | 690.78 | 7689.96 | 2911 |
| 1992-93 | 151 | 802 | 324 | 591.04 | 8953.62 | 2544 |
| 1993-94 | 172 | 970 | 272 | 698.84 | 6692.82 | 2167 |
| 1994-95 | 166 | 1157 | 301 | 1956.32 | 20465.99 | 2839 |
| 1995-96 | 176 | 1467 | 264 | 1715.23 | 23538.84 | 2178 |
| 1996-97 | 199 | 1658 | 92 | 878.00 | 29300.00 | 1968 |
| 1997-98 | 65 | 1388 | 234 | 2100.00 | 11100.00 | 1951 |
| Total | 1124 | 10132 | 5846 | 16022.68 | 174900.39 | 49595 |
| Exponential growth rate | 9.1874 | 8.9223 | | 6.0113 | 5.786 | 0.0844 |
| T. Value | 5.83* | 13.05 | | 4.9* | 4.63* | 0.1 |

*Source :* Compiled from the data provided by Directorate of Industries and Commerce, District Industries Centre and Pondicherry Productivity Council.

* Significant at five percent level.

---

The cumulative figures available up to 1983-84 is taken only to find out the total growth.

for the employment opportunities, in all the other indicators, the growth rate is significant at 1 per cent level. This shows that the entrepreneurship have a positive impact on the industrial growth in Pondicherry.

Another attempt was made to analyse the impact of entrepreneurship on productivity with the help of multiple regression analysis. To test the suitability of this equation, R2 test was also conducted.

**Table 8.3**
**Impact of EDPs on Production**

| *Production* | *Investment* | *Employment* | *EDPs* |
|---|---|---|---|
| 4.3084 | +0.54962 | –0.72359 | +0.26923 |
| | (2.59)** | (1.83)*** | (1.87)*** |
| R2 = 0.6789, F = 10.69* | | | |

* Significant at 5 per cent level
** Significant at 10 per cent level
*** Significant at 25 per cent level

The analysis revealed that the production has been contributed by the investment and the number of entrepreneurial development programmes, but not influenced by the number of persons employed. This may be due to the fact that in large scale industrial units, where production function is carried out with the automation, the increase in labour force may not have a significant influence in the output.

### Impact of Entrepreneurship on Productivity and Exports

Export is another parameter for measuring the economic growth of a country and hence the impact of entrepreneurship was measured in terms of production and export. Since exports could be done only after establishing its own position, Pondicherry started exporting only after the year 1987-88 or the Directorate of Industries and Commerce started recording the exports only from the year 1987-88. Hence the share of exports is presented in the Table 8.4.

The analysis of Table 8.4 reveal that the percentage share of the exports to its production were fluctuation. It was not showing

**Table 8.4**
**Share of Exports in the Production**

| *Year* | *No. of EDPs* | *Annual production (in Lakhs)* | *Exports (Rs. in Crores)* | *Percentage share of Exports* |
|---|---|---|---|---|
| 1987-88 | 18 | 3985.21 | 16.27 | 40.85 |
| 1988-89 | 32 | 6199.33 | 17.04 | 27.49 |
| 1989-90 | 21 | 8905.91 | 28.00 | 31.44 |
| 1990-91 | 26 | 7849.57 | 65.00 | 82.80 |
| 1991-92 | 42 | 7869.96 | 93.00 | 121.00 |
| 1992-93 | 151 | 8953.62 | 120.00 | 134.02 |
| 1993-94 | 172 | 6692.82 | 160.00 | 239.06 |
| 1994-95 | 166 | 20465.99 | 207.00 | 101.01 |
| 1995-96 | 176 | 25538.84 | 240.00 | 101.96 |
| 1996-97 | 199 | 29300.00 | 300.00 | 102.39 |
| 1997-98 | 65 | 11100.00 | 320.00 | 288.29 |
| *Total* | *1068* | *134681.25* | *1566.31* | |
| *Average* | | *12243.75* | *142.39* | *115.48* |

*Source* : Compiled from the data provided by the Directorate of Industries and Commerce, Pondicherry.

any consistent trend. However, it revealed that the export earnings made through the industries of Pondicherry in absolute terms were increasing every year. However, its percentage share was ranging from 27.49 per cent in the year 1988-89 to 288.29 per cent in the year 1997-98. On an average the annual export during this period was Rs.142.39 crores. The percentage share of the exports being more than production may be due to previous years production also.

## Summary

Entrepreneurship has been defined by many economists and others like Joseph Schumpeter, Peter F. Drucker, Walker, William Diamond and Higgins, etc. "It meant the function of seeking investment and production opportunity, organising an enterprise to undertake a new production process, raising capital, hiring labour, arranging the supply of raw materials including new techniques and commodities", etc.

In Pondicherry up to 1954, no systematic efforts were undertaken towards industrial growth, since it was used as a French Trading Centre in India. It is only after its annexation to India (1954) the industrial development was thought of. The Industrial growth started only after establishing Directorate of Industries and Commerce and other infrastructural facilities like Roads, Electricity, work sheds, finance, raw materials and others were made available through various agencies like PIPDIC, NSIC, DIC, etc., apart from the conduct of many entrepreneural development programmes. The industrial growth became prominent only after many incentives and subsidies were made available, considering it as a industrially backward district (1971). Even though all these facilities were provided, industrial growth in its true meaning took place only during and after eighties.

This study reveals that there is growth in the EDPs, growth in the number of industries due to increased EDPs, increase in the output, etc. It further revealed that the impact of EDPs on annual production is significant. The increase in investment also had a positive impact on the production. The increase in employment had no such positive effect on the production.

The other analysis pertaining to EDPs, increase in the industries and exports due to it, revealed that the percentage share of exports were considerable. In some years the exports were more than the annual production due to the previous years production.

On the whole there is a positive impact on the production and employment due to increase in the entrepreneurship. The production per share of investments and employment is more in SSIs than LSIs. Therefore by increasing the number of EDPs and entrepreneurship, the country can be developed at a faster rate.

**References**

1. Gerald M. Meir and Robert E. Baldwin, *Economic Development, Theory, History and Policy*, John Wiley and Sons, New York, 1967, p. 299.
2. Higgins, as quoted in P. Saravana Vel, *Entrepreneurial Development Principles, Policies and Programmes*, Ess Pee Kay Publishing House, Madras 2, 1991, p. 21.

# 9

# Entrepreneurial Remedy for Superfluous Millions

—*Dr. P.S. Tripathi*

Economic growth in true sense involves a sequence of events that lead over a period of time, to economic development and ultimately to the welfare of the people. The rate of growth obtained in an economy is therefore rightly taken as an index of welfare of the people in general. An economy growing at a higher pace is expected to achieve simultaneously the just and equitable distribution of rewards among its factors. The objective of macro economic management is not to attain a higher rate of GDP growth *per se* but to ensure that this leads to increased public welfare. How far, the Indian economy has been able to achieve this goal is a question.

The Human Development Report of UNDP 1996, talks at length, about the phenomenon of Jobless growth particularly in the context of developing countries. It observes: "In Pakistan during the period of 1975 to 1992, real GDP grew by about 6.3 per cent annually but the employment grew only by 2.4 per cent During the same period in India, yearly GDP growth was around 5 per cent while annual growth in employment was around 2 per cent. In Ghana, a stark example, the GDP growth between 1986-91 was 4.8 per cent but employment dropped by more than 13 per cent."

The report further says — "wherever the jobs are created, many are dead-end, Temporary jobs — without security and future. As a result productivity suffered."

"Whatever the cause", the report notes, "We are creating a polarised society in which millions of people are deemed as superfluous". Policies must be re-oriented to boost employment as a top priority. When livelihood in secure society cannot long remain secure.

But herein we should not derive a simplistic conclusion that providing job security by the state will automatically ensure productivity and higher economic growth. Our experience of five decades of performance of Indian Public sector and Indian Planning, in fact, speaks differently. As a welfare state, we enjoined upon us (the state), the responsibility to provide secure livelihood to all able bodied persons, but we have failed miserably in this respect. Not only we in India failed but several other countries of East Europe and erstwhile USSR, working on the similar socialisitic pattern of command and control economy, have met the same fate. As Rudolf H.K. Gultheir observes—

> One of the lessons drawn from the downfall of communism is that in the modern complex world, the top cannot decide what happens on the ground. Many people that think and manage independently are needed to promote innovation and growth. Enablement of such process is the need of the hour.

Similar views were also echoed by Shapiro (1981) when he said—

> A society or community with a high level of entrepreneurship ultimately incurs less risk than the one that relies upon the illusory security of large scale enterprise. For, only a large number of company formations, occurring continuously overtime, can help ensure the creativity and resilience that a community needs to respond to change and capitalise quickly on new opportunities.

Thus, on the one hand, we have the highly technology intensive capitalist system, generating jobless growth and treating the invaluable human resource as unwanted millions and on the other extreme we have the centrally planned systems that lack the sensitivity to ground level dynamics and failed to deliver a sustainable growth. Against the backdrop, rekindling the Individual Enterprise and initiative and creating a network of micro-entrepreneurial ventures (MEVs) across the land, including rural hinterlands; appears an effective remedy. This process will not only increase the inventory of Entrepreneurial talents but will also enhance the employment opportunities manifold in the respective regions. Strategic choice of Entrepreneurial option will reaffirm our faith in what Kautilya said.

It is only the entrepreneurial route that will ensure a just, equitable and sustainable growth in the economy and welfare of the society. Human resource remains our greatest strength and we need to develop a system that allows us to capitalise on this resource and offers independence and innovative freedom with least inertia.

The individual has traditionally formed the focus of our policies whether social, economic or spiritual. The great seer and scholar 'Valluvor' in his famous work *Thirukkural* says

> Industry brings wealth; sloth poverty. The goddess of wealth runs after the man of energy and enterprise and smiles on his home. For the lazy and indolent there is a different visitor — She is the devil of Poverty.

Similar sentiments have also been echoed by Bhartrihari in his famous work 'Neeti Shatakam'—

> We therefore, need entrepreneurs that constitute a vital resource for healthy growth of an economy. We need entrepreneurs to create more jobs in our economy, to introduce innovation, to increase productivity, to reach out new markets, to face growing challenges of international competition, to ensure effective utilisation of scarce resources that are becoming scarce day by day.

### Augmentation of Entrepreneurial Resource

Having established the role of Entrepreneurs in our economy, it is imperative to chalk out an appropriate strategy to support and augment the process of Entrepreneurial growth. A multi-pronged strategy adopted for the purpose may be include *inter alia* —

1. Spotting the existing entrepreneurial talents and inducing them to undertake micro ventures suitable to their own resources and skills supplemented by inputs from support agencies.

2. Crafting a long-term strategy to broadbase the process of Entrepreneurial development and to take remedial measures to overcome the socio-cultural and other barriers that impede the process of growth of Entrepreneurial spirit and entrepreneurs.
3. Creating an integrated package based network of support agencies that are actively involved in nurturing the entrepreneurs. The agencies may involve the promotional institutions like DIC Training Institutions like EDII, IED, TCOs, Management Insititutes, SISI, etc. Institutions offering inputs like power, finance and other support services.
4. Creating clusters of small business enterprises and making them available with advanced R and D, lab testing and standardisation of facilities and helping them in absorption and assimilation of new technology.
5. Providing marketing assistance to small scale enterprises particularly to help the exporting units, numbering about 5000 at present. Further there is a need to evolve a suitable mechanism to promote marketing outlets specialising in marketing the products manufactured by tiny sector. Efforts may also be made to develop a common brand name for such products.

Each of these strategies requires a finer blue print to be worked out further, which we feel is beyond the scope of this chapter.

In conclusion, it may be observed that promotion of Entrepreneurship in right perspective holds the key to solve many of our economic ills and if supported earnestly by input providing agencies, these entrepreneurs could change the face of Indian Economy.

## References

1. *Asian Entrepreneur*, Vol. 1, January-April, 1997.
2. HBR: *Trails and Rewards of the Entrepreneur.*
3. *Entrepreneurs Embattled*: Gillian Godsell
4. *Entrepreneurship in India's Small Scale Industries*, Richard, P. Taub, Doris, L. Taub.
5. *Executive Summary*—Report of the Expert Committee on Small Enterprises, 1997.
6. *Human Development Report*, UNDP, 1996.

# 10

# Entrepreneurship Marketing

*—V. Balakrishnan*

## Introduction

Enterpreneurship Marketing is a new concept offering different strategic emphasis in identification, competence building, problem solving and technology orientation, in the process of creating new Entrepreneurs. It can be defined as a concept marketing process through credible source with stress on empathy to spread industrial culture by providing education, information exposure on technology and market infrastructural facilities, investment options and imbibing the intricacies of business. The sustained supply of Entrepreneurs with high level of survival rate is the unique feature of this concept.

## Hypothesis

The concept was developed through interaction with academicians, industrialists, emerging Entrepreneurs and institutions involved in industrial finance. It was validated through model building and testing if in a urban node which is not exposed to industrial activities. A survey to identify the factors that inhibit the transformation of job seekers to Entrepreneurs was conducted among 1860 educated. The same included unemployed persons, 200 traders, 200 Agriculturists, 100 under-employed professionals and 50 members involved in Entrepreneur building activity.

The Government Agencies were roped in the process of implementing the infrastructural development process. A survey was conducted through interview method among 50 transformed Entrepreneurs.

**General Discussion**

This research brings forth use of inadequacies of organization oriented Entrepreneur Development Programmes. As the Entrepreneurship Marketing is customer oriented, it will generate more Entrepreneurs to the economy.

The growth of Entrepreneurs in any society will widen the tax base resulting in generation of Revenue for the Government, creation of more employment opportunities, information explosion of technology sources, induction of innovative and inventive spirit and identified investment options. The society will derive the benefit of acquiring products at competitive prices and better standard of living. The indulgence in anti-social activities due to unemployment can be minimised.

The Entrepreneurship marketing can be done at three levels. At primary level the younger generation can be educated about Entrepreneurship at the school level for breaking the job seeking cultural behaviour. Next at the secondary level dissemination meets can be organized to target audience for imbibing the fruits of creation of Entrepreneurs. In the final phase credible source can market Entrepreneurship as intervention strategy to identify and develop Entrepreneurs. At this stage a problem resolution mechanism can be created for retaining the entrepreneur character among newly created industrialists. It becomes imperative for the Government to reorient the functions of its agencies involved in industrial infrastructural development as consumer oriented rather than working as an outfit carrying on bureaucratic legacy.

Under the new concept the product Entrepreneurship has to be perfected as quality product. In this process delivering updated information at call is the basic service the target audience expects in addition to assurance, reliability, responsiveness, empathy and availability of infrastructural facilities at minimum cost. Though the target audience look for stability and sustained growth, at the entry level, investment on non-productive assets are to be kept at the lowest level. The distribution of this concept can be done through Non-Governmental Organization, rendering real service and through professional consultants and corporate bodies delinked from the power base of the government. As regards promotion, publicity and public relations are best vehicles rather than advertising.

The model tested in an urban node among the target audience comprising of traders, educated unemployed youth, alternate income searching agriculturist and under-employed professionals yield overwhelming response. This model suits very well for small scale entrepreneurs. Marketing Entrepreneurship among large scale, medium scale and tiny sector Entrepreneurs have different target audience and hence a variation in the model can be adopted for achieving the desired goal.

The Prime Minister's Rozgar Yojana is the best model for Entrepreneurship Marketing to tiny Sector, but to be delinked from bureaucratic outfits.

## Conclusions

The Entrepreneurship marketing is a successful concept marketing tool available in the knit of Governments for massive industrialization. In this process professional and not bureaucrats are to be involved. The problem resolution mechanism must carry empathy and made as a permanent body. It establishes that Entrepreneurship Marketing is incongruent to Entrepreneur Development in approach, process and results. It will produce certain highly visible results in Entrepreneur generation.

## References

1. Berry L.Leonard, Zeithami A. Velarie and A. Parasuraman, "Five Imperatives for Improving Service Quality", *Sloan Management Review*, Vol. 31, No. 4, Summer, 1990.
2. Howard Brich, Philipkoteer, "A Framework for Marketing Image Management", *Sloan Management Review*, Vol. 12, No. 12, Winter, 1991.
4. Prahlad C.K. and Gary Hamel, *The Core Competence of the Corporation*, HBR, No. 3, May-June, 1990.

# 11

# Rural Women Entrepreneurs: Problems and Prospects

—*Dr. A.K. Choudhary*
—*Dr. S.C. Sharma*

When a woman moves forward, the family moves and the village moves and the nation moves. Upliftment of women is an essential ingredient of human development. Entrepreneurship development among the rural women force would strengthen the village economy and promote regional development.

The 1991 National Sample Survey figures show that women share only 14.1 per cent of employment of total employment and only a meagre 5.6 per cent of them are employed in government jobs. In the rural sector 56 per cent of the males and 33 per cent of females are in the labour force. From the opposite angle we see that 66 per cent of the female labour in the rural sector is idle, unutilised.

This is mainly due to existing social customs putting men and women on different footings.

Women are usually not able to take benefit of the employment schemes, specially those of self-employment because of huge unemployment in male youth and employment for man is being considered more necessary than for women, who are seen only as Supplementary earners.

Young unmarried girls are normally not allowed to work independently. Women are mostly illiterate and unaware and cannot find their way in the maze of formalities involved in getting employment in job creating schemes specially self employment.

Rural women possess all qualities to be entrepreneurs still they lack confidence in their ability to run the enterprise especially at the beginning stage.

Rural women are not so aware and literate as to handle all the legal and other formalities in loan taking and establishing an industrial unit. They have to work in a men-dominated social environment and still the men have not fully accepted the efficiency of women.

But now the scenario is fast changing with modernisation, urbanisation and development of education and business. Thus the opportunities of employment for women have increased drastically. It is found that the percentage of unemployment among educated and qualified women is increasing. Thus it is necessary to increase the opportunity of self-employment for educated unemployed women through the development of entrepreneurship. It should be stated here that the self-employed entrepreneur creates not only her employment but also creates employment opportunities to others.

It is most important to create a favourable atmosphere for a healthy development of women entrepreneurship. We have an example of Kerala of how the women entrepreneurs have responded to their work in a favourable atmosphere since last two decades. In 1975-76, the number of industrial units of women entrepreneurs were 73 in Kerala. They have increased to 4190 Industrial Units in 1993-94. The women entrepreneurs in Kerala are now at the top of all industries from readymade garments to high-tech computers.

**Rural Development Programmes**

The main objective of Integrated Rural Development Programme is to increase the income generating power of the families who are below the poverty line. Thirty per cent women should be the beneficiaries in Rural Development Programme run by the government. The main rural development programmes are:

**Indira Mahila Yojana (IMY)**

IMY was launched in August, 1995. Its main objective is to give a forward thrust to education, awareness, income generation capacity and empowerment to women. The platform for the forward thrust is to be done through self-help groups at the grassroots level.

**Rashtriya Mahila Kosh (RMK)**

RMK was established in 1992 with a fund of Rs. 31 crore to meet the needs of poor women by giving them loans. RMK is also organising training, apprenticeship and orientation programmes for trainers under the Indian Mahila Block Societies (IMBS). The objective of RMK is that credit becomes a widely known and used facility for enhancement of the daily income of poor women. The experience of RMK is that the women would have been able to double or triple their daily income with the credit support of Rs. 2500 or Rs. 5000. The activities followed may be dairying, petty shop keeping and investment on the agricultural operations.

RMK has disbursed Rs. 16 crores out of the sanctioned credit limit of Rs. 26 crores and the recovery is 92 per cent consequently for the last three years. This only proves that poor women are extremely creditworthy if NGO's give them the necessary support and guidance.

**Step**

Step was started in 1987 with the objective to provide training to rural women for increasing their production capacity and income generation. In this programme, they give training in the areas of traditional business like—agriculture, milk, fisheries, Handlooms, Khadi development, etc.

2.5 lakh women have been benefitted by the programme since its inception. Maximum number of beneficiaries are of milk producing area. In 1996-97 (Up to 31st December 1996), this programme has an expenditure of 1.44 crore and the number of women beneficiaries are 2400.

**NORAD Programme**

NORAD (Norwegian Agency for International Development) was established in 1982-83 to help the educated and uneducated women financially in non-traditional areas of business like electronics, computer programming, manufacturing of watches, printing, readymade garments, etc.

64,200 women were benefitted by NORAD programme. In 1996-97 (up to 31st December 1996), it has an expenditure of 335.91 lakhs and the beneficiary women are 6065.

**ARVIND**

The National Bank for Agriculture and Rural Development (NABARD) has started a rural women development programme called ARVIND. It provides loan up to Rs. 10 lakhs to the women who work collectively in agriculture for their economic development.

**DWCRA**

DWCRA is the Rural Development Department's Scheme to support women's income generation activities through a group of 15 to 20 women each. The government of India has launched this women and children development programme in 1982. The main objective of this programme is to strengthen the economy of rural women by giving them loan and economic assistance to develop their skills, efficiency and abilities to meet their liabilities effectively.

**TRYSEM**

TRYSEM is a sub-plan of Integrated Rural Development programme. It gives training to the young unemployed men and women for self-employment. The trainees get a stipend of Rs. 150 per month during training period. In this programme 40 per cent of total seats are reserved for women. About 16 lakh women have been trained from its inception till now.

**Young Beneficiaries under TRYSEM**

*(in Lakh)*

| *Year* | *Target* | *Achievement* |
|---|---|---|
| 1992-93 | 3.00 | 2.76 |
| 1993-94 | 3.50 | 3.04 |
| 1994-95 | 3.18 | 2.84 |
| 1995-96 | 2.16 | 2.87 |

The Nationalised Banks have also given special attention for the development of the women entrepreneurs in recent years.

This is really an encouraging and inducing step as it was neglected earlier.

The services of Gram Sevikas, SWCRA leaders/members, Panchayat members should be utilised to create awareness among women about the advantages and incentives involved in the scheme.

**Conclusion**

The Ninth plan has given priority to agriculture and rural development with a view to generate adequate protective employment.

The Union Budget 1998-99, has also increased the budget for rural development by 6.4 per cent, i.e, 7691 crores in 1997-98 to 8182 crores in 1998-99.

In recent years, the self-employment opportunities are most popular with rural women. They can start poultry, dairy, piggeries, bee keeping, goatry, petty shop keeping, agriculture and allied operations and establish small units to produce pickle, papad, sauce and other similar products in collective way. Easy facilitation of credit through BMK and IMBS can go a long way in ensuring this. NGO's wherever working, should motivate women to become entrepreneurs — appropriate training is needed in various developmental activities and programmes so that they can improve their knowledge, attitude and skills to perform their jobs efficiently and effectively. This should include vocational training for income generating activities and training to develop self-confidence to take up entrepreneurship. The only urgent need is to create a favourable atmosphere to increase self-employment among women to cope up with the overall development of the country. Women employment is the felt need of the day in our country and a separate package is needed to develop entrepreneurship among rural women.

# 12

# Problems of Women Entrepreneurs in Chennai: A Pilot Study

*—Dr. N.P. Srinivasan*
*—Dr. R. Sreenivasagalu*

*All Nations have achieved greatness by paying proper respect to women. That country and that Nation which do not respect women have never become great, nor will ever be in future.*

—Swami Vivekananda

Today our government is more concerned about the overall economic development of women and for this, development of "Entrepreneurship" among women has become an important aspect of plan priorities. A broad-based organisational arrangement for disseminating information, conducting women oriented programmes by Banks and Financial institutions, better linkage between Institute of Entrepreneurship Development and the Entrepreneurship Association at state level could pave the way for speedy development in this direction.

Women entrepreneurs in India represent a group of women who have broken away from the beaten trade and are exploring new avenues of economic participation. Their tasks have been full of challenges. They have had to encounter public prejudices and criticism. Family opposition and social constraints had to be overcome before establishing themselves as Independent entrepreneurs.

Establishing and managing an industrial unit or business requires more effort, skill and risk. The risk can be both Financially and Emotionally very high. For the women entrepreneur the risk perhaps is even greater as she has the additional problems of being in a male dominated society, having few role models and lacking confidence in her business skills.

In spite of so many hurdles and limitations, the participation of women in Entrepreneurial activities is steadily increasing. The government has recognised this particular section as a source of potential entrepreneurs and also as a special target group to develop. Accordingly different developmental agencies have come up to assist them.

Since this group is treated as a under-privileged section of the society in terms of their behaviour, character skills and problems, there is a need to study the different problems faced by them and the remedial measures required for promoting women entrepreneurs.

This study is on Problems of women entrepreneurs in Chennai.

**Objectives**

*(i)* To Analyse and critically examine the problems faced by the women entrepreneurs.

*(ii)* To suggest different remedial measures in helping and promoting women entrepreneurship.

**Methodology**

The present study was carried out in Chennai city of Tamilnadu selecting 50 women entrepreneurs, doing different types of business. The data for the study was mainly collected through a structured schedule and personal interview. The information was collected on the following:

*(i)* Problems faced by them.

*(ii)* Remedial measures required.

**Problems**

Entrepreneurship is not a 'bed of Roses' to the women. Their task has become more tedious and full of challenges since they have to encounter public prejudices and criticism. Women face certain problems not as a entrepreneur but as a woman. Therefore, when compared to men the problems of women entrepreneurs are more in number.

Problems faced by women entrepreneurs were classified as under:

1. Socio-personal problems.
2. Managerial problems.
3. Production problems.
4. Marketing problems.
5. Financial problems.
6. Problems of Government assistance.

### *1. Socio-personal Problems*

Most of the women are facing the problem of wrong attitude of the society against them. In a male dominated society, women are encountered with many socio-personal problems. These problems can be seen from Table 12.1.

**Table 12.1**
**Socio-Personal Problems**

| *Problems* | *Numbers* | *Percentage* |
|---|---|---|
| 1. Lack of family and community support | 35 | 70 |
| 2. Male dominated society | 30 | 60 |
| 3. Lack of Education and Information | 25 | 50 |
| 4. Economic Backwardness | 25 | 50 |
| 5. Low Risk bearing capacity | 20 | 50 |

*Note:* Data indicates multiple responses.

It is seen from the Table 12.1 that 70 per cent of the respondents are not getting family and community support. 60 per cent of them are facing the problem of male domination in the society and in the business world. 50 per cent of them are facing the problem of illiteracy and economic backwardness. Only 40 per cent of them stated the problem of low risk bearing capacity.

### 2. *Managerial Problems*

Managerial problems are another important problems stated by most of the respondents. Most of the respondents did not have knowledge of General Management and Labour administration. Majority of them did not have clear-cut objectives for their business enterprise. These problems can be seen from Table 12.2.

**Table 12.2**
**Managerial Problems**

| *Problems* | *Numbers* | *Percentage* |
|---|---|---|
| 1. Lack of knowledge of General Management and Experience | 30 | 60 |
| 2. Lack of skilled labour | 26 | 52 |
| 3. Labour Absenteeism and Labour turnover | 26 | 52 |
| 4. Lack of Clearcut objectives | 25 | 50 |
| 5. Transportation problem as women | 23 | 46 |

*Note:* Data indicates multiple responses.

It is seen from the Table 12.2 that 60 per cent of the respondents are facing the problem of lack of knowledge of general management and experience. 52 per cent of them are facing the problem of lack of skilled labour, labour absenteeism and labour turnover. 50 per cent of them stated that they did not have any clear-cut objectives for their business enterprise. 46 per cent of them are facing the problem of transportation as women for procurement of inputs and to market their products.

### 3. *Production Problems*

These problems are encountered by the women entrepreneurs during production process. These problems can be seen from Table 12.3.

It is seen from the Table 12.3 that 70 per cent of the respondents did not have adequate land, plots and premises for production process. 66 per cent of them are facing the problems of getting required inputs for production. 58 per cent of them stated that they did not get adequate technical support for product identification and machinery utilisation. 50 per cent of them are facing problems of lack of upgradation of Technology and Research and Development. Only 48 per cent of them stated that they have poor inventory management.

**Table 12.3**
**Production Problems**

| *Problems* | *Numbers* | *Percentage* |
|---|---|---|
| 1. Inadequate availability of land, plots and premises | 35 | 70 |
| 2. Problem of getting required inputs | 33 | 66 |
| 3. Inadequate Technical support of product indentification and machinery utilisation | 29 | 58 |
| 4. Lack of upgradation of Technology, Research and Development and Quality Control | 25 | 50 |
| 5. Poor Inventory Management | 24 | 48 |

*Note:* Data indicates multiple responses.

### 4. *Marketing Problems*

Now-a-days marketing problem is common to all entrepreneurs. Most of them find it difficult to market their products. They do not possess the knowledge of how to market their products and whom to contact for the purpose. As women they face these marketing problems still more. These problems can be seen from Table 12.4.

**Table 12.4**
**Marketing Problems**

| *Problems* | *Numbers* | *Percentage* |
|---|---|---|
| 1. Lack of knowledge of how to market the product and whom to contact | 38 | 76 |
| 2. Heavy competition with Big enterprises | 31 | 62 |
| 3. Exploitation by middlemen and Difficulties in collection of dues | 28 | 56 |
| 4. Inadequate sales promotion avenues | 27 | 54 |
| 5. Lack of Export marketing support | 25 | 50 |

*Note:* Data indicates multiple responses.

From the Table 12.4 it is seen that 76 per cent of the

respondents did not know how to market their products. 62 per cent of them are facing heavy competition from big enterprises. 56 per cent of them stated that they are exploited by middlemen and find difficulty in collection of dues from credit sales. 54 per cent of them stated that they are not having adequate sales promotion avenues. 50 per cent of them stated that they did not get any Export marketing support.

### 5. *Financial Problems*

Financial problem is a major problem faced by all entrepreneurs. Finance is essential to start as well as to run a business enterprise. Most of the women entrepreneurs are facing financial problems at the time of starting as well as during operation of their business enterprises. These problems can be seen from Table 12.5.

**Table 12.5**
**Financial Problems**

| *Problems* | *Numbers* | *Percentage* |
|---|---|---|
| 1. Problem of getting loan and subsidy | 37 | 74 |
| 2. Insistence or collateral and margin money requirement | 32 | 64 |
| 3. Time taken to process loan | 26 | 52 |
| 4. Tight repayment schedule | 26 | 52 |
| 5. Poor Financial Management and maintenance of accounts | 21 | 42 |

*Note:* Data indicates multiple responses.

It is seen from Table 12.5 that 74 per cent of the respondents find it difficult to get the required loan and subsidy in time. 64 per cent of them did not have collateral and margin money requirement. 52 per cent of them stated that more time is taken to process the loan and complained tight repayment schedule. Only 42 per cent of them did not have proper financial management and did not maintain proper accounts.

### 6. *Problems of Government Assistance*

Both Central and State Governments are implementing various

assistance schemes for promotion of women entrepreneurship. But in practice women entrepreneurs are facing many difficulties in obtaining various government assistances. These problems can be seen from Table 12.6.

**Table 12.6**
**Problems of Government Assistance**

| Problems | Numbers | Percentage |
|---|---|---|
| 1. Inadequate Government assistance | 35 | 70 |
| 2. Red Tapism at various levels | 30 | 60 |
| 3. Advisory organisations become exploitive and dishonest | 28 | 76 |
| 4. Complicated and time consuming procedures for getting the assistance | 24 | 48 |
| 5. Government policies are not favourable | 22 | 44 |

*Note:* Data indicates multiple responses

From Table 12.6 it is seen that 70 per cent of the respondents feel that Government assistance is not adequate for them. 60 per cent of them stated that Red Tapism is prevailing at various levels. 56 per cent of them stated that Advisory organisations are exploitive and dishonest. 48 per cent of them stated the problem of complicated and time consuming procedures in getting the assistance, 44 per cent of them feel that Government policies are not favourable and encouraging for them.

The above said 6 problems are ranked and shown in Table 12.7.

**Table 12.7**
**Problems of Women Entrepreneurs**

| Problems | Percentage | Rank |
|---|---|---|
| 1. Financial Problems | 90 | 1 |
| 2. Marketing Problems | 85 | 2 |
| 3. Production Problems | 75 | 3 |
| 4. Socio-Personal Problems | 65 | 4 |
| 5. Problems of Government assistance | 60 | 5 |
| 6. Managerial Problems | 50 | 6 |

From Table 12.7 it is seen that financial problems ranked first followed by marketing problems, production problems, socio-personal problems, problems of Government assistance and managerial problems.

**Remedial Measures in Assisting and Promoting Women Entrepreneurship**

To widen and strengthen the base of women entrepreneurship the following Remedial measures may prove meaningful:

1. To solve financial problems, Government and Financial institutions should draw and implement special lending policies like waiving of collecteral and margin money requirements, quick processing of loan and liberal repayment schedule for women entrepreneurs. Government and other voluntary organisations should conduct financial Management training programme for women entrepreneurs.
2. To solve the marketing problems Government and voluntary organisations should conduct elaborate marketing training to women entrepreneurs. The government should give subsidies and concessions to women entrepreneurs to face price competition from big enterprises. It is suggested that the government should make reservation of certain products to women entrepreneurs. Government and women entrepreneurs association should make arrangement for conducting Exhibitions and conferences of women entrepreneurs. Government should also establish a women entrepreneur's shopping complex for marketing their products.
3. Attention of the government should be drawn in rectifying the production problems by the allotment of factory shed and land in government industrial estates on priority basis, supply of raw materials and other inputs regularly at subsidised rates, giving assistance for upgradation of technology, research and development and giving production training to women entrepreneurs.
4. Attention of the government as well as voluntary organisations need to be drawn to rectify socio-personal problems. A special programme can be conducted against the social evils. Liberal assistance and gearing up of various facilities should be done for enhancement of the status of women entrepreneurs.

To solve the problems of getting government assistance, it is recommended that adequate assistance should be given to the right person at the right time. A special advisory organisation should be established. Simplified procedures should be followed in getting the government assistance. Government officials should show favourable attitude towards women entrepreneurs.

## Conclusion

The growth of industrialisation, education and domestic system has brought about significant changes in the tradition bound Indian Society. Now increasing proportion of women are seeking gainful employment in industrial field. They are also successfully in modern sophisticated industries like electronics, engineering and consultancy. However, the movement of women entrepreneurs development is still in a transitional phase. They have yet a long way to be on par with their male partners. A comprehensive entrepreneurship development programme would help a lot in this direction if dealt with all seriousness and sincerity. It is a fact that man alone cannot break the evils of poverty, unemployment and inequality. Active and equal participation of women is indispensible in fighting against these social-evils.

## References

1. *"Women Entrepreneurs in India"* –Medha Dubhashi Vinze.
2. *"Developing New Entrepreneurs" – EDII.* Ahmedabad, 1987.
3. *"Developing of Women Entrepreneurship"* – Sudarshan Sahoo – Khadigramodyog, Nov. 1991.
4. *"A Profile of Potential Rural Women Entrepreneurs"* – V. Jyothi and G. Prasad, *SEDME*, Vol. XX(1).
5. *Problems of Women Entrepreneurs in Agra*—Dr. Shalini Nigam.
6. Hisrich, R.D.L. "The Women Entrepreneurs : Characteristics, Skills, Problems and Prescriptions for Success", in *The Art and Science of Entrepreneurship,* Mass Ballingar Publishing Co.

# 13

# Problems of Women Entrepreneurs as Revealed by Them

—*Dr. S. Ganesan*
—*Mr. R. Duraipandian*

The traditional perception of women as a helper in the occupation of the husband and a home-maker is gradually vanishing in the recent past. Women have started proving themselves in many fields including entrepreneurship and their participation in entrepreneurial activities has increased by leaps and bound. Quite a large number of women entrepreneurs have set up their enterprises and have been in business successfully. Though majority of women entrepreneurs work at either micro level or tiny/cottage sectors, presence of women as owners in large scale enterprises is not uncommon.

The realisation that women are a valuable human resource has been gaining around. They play a crucial role in human development through child rearing and support services at home. Recognition of women's services as a necessary sub-system of the entire socio-economic system is gradually becoming a part of modern attitudes.

Many factors and developments have influenced women to take up entrepreneurship. The success of White Revolution has identified the closeness of women to animal husbandry. In most of the states, particularly in Gujarat, women own a majority of milch animals. The advent of labour saving technology is another very important socio-economic development. Such technology frees women from the drudgery of long labour. The acceptance of the small family concept and the resultant break-up of traditional joint family system have resulted in psychological liberation experienced by women. The successive industrial policies of the government have laid greater emphasis on the development of women entrepreneurship in the country. A large number of entrepreneurship development programmes especially for women have been conducted over the years, thus motivating women to become entrepreneurs. A related development is the introduction of special cells and schemes by financial institutions for catering to the financial needs of prospective women entrepreneurs. Improved level of women education has increased the aspirations to widen their horizon and extend their role. More women, now, opt for higher technical and professional education as the educational facilities are increasing in the country. Proportion of women in the labour force has also increased as a result of this. All these factors and developments have influenced women to take up non-traditional higher levels of activities (like that of entrepreneurship) apart from their conventional role of home making.

The Alagappa Institute of Management has taken up a major research project to identify the motivational factors and to assess the success rate of women entrepreneurs in Tamilnadu. As a part of the project, the Institute organised a Focus Group meeting of women entrepreneurs. The meeting, which was attended by 16 women entrepreneurs, provided a lot of information on the motivational factors, style of functioning, and problems faced by them. This chapter discusses the problems faced by the women entrepreneurs, heavily drawing information provided at the Focus Group Meeting.

## Problems Faced by Women Entrepreneurs

The problems faced by women entrepreneurs in the country emanate from a multitude of sources and are manifold. These problems can be classified under three broad categories, viz., personal, social and economic.

### Personal Problems

The lack of experience, lack of adequate technical knowledge, lack of business exposure, and conservative attitude towards risk taking are some of the personal problems of women entrepreneurs. Women have been traditionally doing the service jobs in business enterprises. Back home, they have been involved only in activities concerning home making. A majority of the households do not consult women in major decisions resulting in a situation where women lacked experience in managing major problems individually. Another related problem is the lack of adequate technical knowledge on the part of women. Humanities and arts programmes have traditionally been in great demand by women students. Women students were not encouraged to take up technical programmes as the society was of the opinion that the women were not suitable to such programmes. Woman in general, seem to have a conservative attitude towards family and business. It is hard to convince an average woman to accept to changes. This quality of risk and change aversion worked against women in their development.

Added to all these, are the physiological problems women face. The fragile structure of the body, mensuration, pregnancy, need to tender infants, and the likes are some of the problems specific to women. Working women have the option of taking leave subject to limitations — when they face such "problems". Women entrepreneurs cannot afford to go on leave during the crucial phases of the ventures.

**Social Problems**

Women in general face a lot of problems in the male dominated society. There are many unwritten rules, which the society scrupulously follows. Most of these rules pertain to women and encompass a wide variety of social activities like women's interaction with others, women's education, their employment, hours of work, dress outings, and the like. Women can interact only with known persons. The society talks ill of a woman who moves freely with "outsiders". The situation is not uncommon even in metropolitan cities of the country. Women find it difficult to have even business relationship with "others" due to hostile social environment. There may not be any difficulty for women entrepreneurs who operate on a large scale in an organised sector because they can afford to employ professional executives for taking care of the business operations. Moreover, the society accepts the violation of social norms by women in the higher echelons of the society. Similarly, the women entrepreneurs operating at micro level — like street vendors, petty shop owners, etc.– do have very less problems with the society, as the society does not care about them. It is only the women at the middle level who faces a lot of problems in their professions or enterprises. Society seems to be very harsh to women at the middle level.

Most women do not have their own choice even in the matter of education. A large proportion of rural girls drop out from schooling in their early ages. The choice of educational programmes of the middle class women is restricted to arts and humanities subjects. Even those who venture out of professional programmes in engineering and technology have difficulty in getting suitable employment commensurate with their education. Instances of technically qualified women taking up employment at clerical level are very common.

**Employment**

While men do not have much problem in taking up employment of their choice, women in India and other Asian countries face lot of problems in getting suitable employment. The organisations prefer women to be employed at staff level. Very less number of women are employed at the executive level. Moreover women cannot have free mobility to take up employment at far away places. All this have resulted in a societal belief that women are suitable only for providing service to the men dominated societal systems. When a woman dares to enter into a technology driven entrepreneurial venture, she faces many impediments even in the normal course of management of the enterprise.

**Hours of Work**

Women are considered as the weaker sex and subtle. There is also a belief that women cannot withstand longer hours of work, and works at odd hours. This environment is not congenial to women to take up those entrepreneurial ventures, which demand lot of their time at odd hours. Women here can become successful entrepreneurs only when either they have an enabling workforce behind them or the venture itself can be taken care of at their own time.

**Economic Problems**

Till recently the women in India did not have legal rights in their parental properties. The women had to satisfy with the Sthridhan provided to them at the time of their marriage. The relevant Act has now been amended to recognise the rights of women in the parental properties. However, the change in the legal framework in favour of women sharing family property with their brothers has not been recognised in the major part of the country. Women could not provide any collateral security for their loans in the absence of any property. This presented women in poor light in the eyes of the banking system. The banks insist on the husband's or father's signature on the documents, when a woman applies for loan. Women in India and many of the developing countries face innumerable problems, as they do not possess any economic power.

Development of entrepreneurship among women in our country heavily depends on removing all the above personal, social, and economic problems. Most of these problems could not be solved within a short period, since they involve changing the societal values and traditions with respect to women. The government can take up some of the economic problems immediately for their redressal. The society and the government have to undertake many concerted efforts before an enabling environment is created for developing women entrepreneurs in large number.

# 14

# The Dilemma of Entrepreneurial Education

*—Dr. R.K. Pandey*

## Introduction

Whenever in the history of mankind, some knowledge, skills and traits appeared to be gainful and rewarding, human race has rigorously attempted to indoctrinate, imbibe and instil them. May it be the concept of bravery during the days of kingdoms, may it be virtue of philosophical thinking during renaissance period, may it be values of scientific attitude and temper in the era of industrial revolution or may it be the significance of entrepreneurship in today's economic systems when, virtually all the economies are hankering for right people to rejuvenate themselves. Although, the styles of nurturing the desired characteristics, in the past, have been different in different societies, their cardinal principle behind the inculcation processes, remained fundamentally the same. It was based on the concept of experiential transfer through the experienced mentors and gurus to the people already having right orientations. The society had recognised the significance of experience in making the teaching — learning transmissions quick, complete and meaningful: it did not encourage professionalism of articulated speech for imparting skills and knowledge. They knew that it is the experience which adds substance and makes the communications meaningful and not the words and style of the language. Even in today's context, the best documents for management education are mostly produced by the experienced managers from the days of Fayol, Taylor and Bernard till recent years and seldom by the professional authors. These preliminary deliberations on entrepreneurial resource development perplex some basic questions about the entrepreneurial education :

*(a)* Who should be entrusted the responsibility of entrepreneurial education? Successful Entrepreneurs or professional teachers?
*(b)* Should one look into some pre-requisites of traits and personality factors into a novice before grooming him into an entrepreneur? Or are our scientific education methods powerful enough to develop anyone into an entrepreneur?
*(c)* Should the methods of entrepreneurial education be explicit and formal? Or should it be made implicit by way of self-rewarding?
*(d)* What should be the role of support systems?

Most of the institutions of technology and management, all over the world, under pressing demand of their respective economies, have plunged into the business of entrepreneurial education since last one decade without caring of these basic questions. And, like a good business organisation, some of them assertively publish for having contributed a significant number of entrepreneurs. Their claim, however, appears to be more akin to those of mushroomed competition — coaching centres and announcing some kind of relationship with all those who have been successful in the competitive examinations.

An examination of concept of entrepreneurship is essential before pondering into the performance of these institutions.

### The Meaning of Entrepreneurship

Economists and management educators acknowledge J.B. Say for having coined the word entrepreneurship almost two hundred years ago. The meaning of the term, in the sense of its originator, is *the ability to take the factors of production — land, labour and capital — and use them to produce new goods and services.* Subsequently, the meaning of this word was enlarged and specified in the light of different economic theories, as the role of an entrepreneur remained pivotal for economic production in almost all theories.

For example, Schumpeter (1934) visualised entrepreneur primarily as an innovator whose novel productivity might be manifested in five ways:

1. The introduction of a new good — that is one with which consumers are not yet familiar — or a new quality of goods.
2. The introduction of a new method of production, that is one not yet tested by experience in the branch of manufacture concerned, which need by no means be founded upon a discovery scientifically, new, and can also exist in a new way of handling a commodity commercially.
3. The opening of a new market, that is a market into which the particular branch of manufacture of the country in question has not previously entered, whether or not this market has existed before.
4. The conquest of a new source of supply of raw materials or half manufactured goods, again irrespective of whether this source already existed or whether it first has to be created.
5. The carrying out of the new organisation of any industry, like the creation of a monopoly situation or breaking up of a monopoly position.

Management gurus, whose prime focus is narrowed down to business ventures, look at the entrepreneurship differently. Peter F. Drucker (1986) for example, conceives that the "entrepreneur always searches for change, responds to it, and exploits it as an opportunity." Jules Backman (1983) thinks that, "basically, the entrepreneur sees a need and then brings together the manpower, materials, and capital required to meet the need." Many other additions for manoeuring the meaning of entrepreneurship has been done by the business-management experts in their own contexts. All of them amount to say that an entrepreneur is one who ventures a new business or tries to improve the organisational system by initiating productive changes. Entrepreneurial process is discontinuous for it inherently welcomes newness in the scheme of the productive process.

Behaviour scientists talk about entrepreneurship in terms of skills and personality attributes. According to them an entrepreneur is one who,

1. takes initiative for actions that go beyond their job

requirements or the demand of the situation,

2. thinks creatively for innovating the process of production and searching new markets,
3. takes risks in making pragmatic decisions,
4. looks for and takes action on opportunities,
5. takes persistent action to overcome obstacles that get in the way of reaching goals,
6. takes action for clarifying problems through information generation,
7. acts to beat the existing standards of excellence,
8. has a strong belief in self and own abilities, building in high level of self-confidence,
9. capable of solving the problems by switching to an alternate strategy or generating new solutions,
10. successfully persuades others,
11. commands effective inter-personal skills for influencing people,
12. capable of confronting the problems directly and asserting his solution to the people involved,
13. possesses overall conceptual skill, and
14. usually concerned for the people with whom he works.

Instilling these skills should be the prime tasks of the institutes assuming the responsibility of entrepreneurial education: Is it possible within the existing framework of formal education programmes? What would be its effectiveness?

Amidst the aforesaid jungle of varying and many western ideas about entrepreneurhship, we tend to forget that economic welfare of the people ought to have been the basic concern of every society. And, as the entrepreneurial activities are pivotal to all the economic processes, every socio-cultural set-up must have recognised and said something about entrepreneurship in one form or the other.

The Indian wise, in their traditional style of *Sutra* like expressions have condensed the entire extended meanings and senses of entrepreneurial activities in one word *'Uddyam'*. This word combines two syllables, the prefix UT and the YAM. YAM refers to the boundary of systems—behaviour made by norms, rules, methods, procedures and other design characteristics that makes system to exist but develops intertia into the system. It refers to all types of systems, whether economic, social or ecological. And UT connotes the sense of transgression or enhancement of the system boundary. Hence *Uddyam*, in its true sense, means all human endeavours that tend to break the inertia and transgress the boundary of the systems. Whether it is a matter of originating business or subsequent expansion, whether it is the job of combining factors of production or whether it is the task of changing processes, products and markets, nothing can happen without breaking the existing network of inertia in the system. To do so, a person is bound to be innovative, creative, persistent, self-confident, efficiency oriented, assertive and persuasive. These characteristics are natural requirements of *Uddyam*.

Further, in a shloka the chief characteristics of the people, engaged in *Uddyam*, have been identified by Indian wise with such a confidence that at the end of shloka they say, "Wealth searches the house of these people to live in." The first characteristic is that the person should be fervent and full of enthusiasm so that his latent energy can be brought to action, he should be efficient especially for time resource input because it is time dimension which adds value to all other resources, he should have conceptual skill of all the processes and methods where he is going to break the inertia, his mind should not be conditioned in worldly habits to enable him to think a new way, he should be brave so that he may assert his new ways and methods, he should possess a deep sense of obligation to ensure and encourage a continued support of the people with whom he works, he should be firm and persistent for consummating the efforts, and he should be compassionate and humane so that he may have a regular source of inspiration for remaining engaged in different *Uddyam*.

While giving a glimpse of the Indian vision of entrepreneurship, it was not an intention to establish the supremacy of Indian thinking over westerners, rather the inclination was to open the vision for better understanding of the concept.

The question arises: May we really indoctrinate and inculcate the entrepreneurial skills through formal education in institutes by lectures and project assignment methods? Are we honest in this regard? Let us examine what efforts are being made by the institutes engaged in imparting entrepreneurial skills.

## The Entrepreneurial Education Scenario

Kao and Dana (1992) made an extensive study and examination of 300 course outlines of entrepreneurial education run at different universities and institutes all over the world, and categorised them according to their orientation and emphasis. The major thrust of the subject-matter for entrepre-neurial development were: entrepreneurial culture, entrepre-neurial behaviour, entrepreneurial skills, enterprise culture and small business management. Different institutions had different stress on the area. The curriculum of these courses, in general, embodied:

(*a*) Concept of entrepreneurship
(*b*) Entrepreneurship theory
(*c*) Process of entrepreneurship and entrepreneurial life path
(*d*) Entrepreneurial skills and traits
(*e*) Enterprise formation and development
(*f*) Opportunity identification and assessment
(*g*) Methods of resource acquisition
(*h*) Legal environment of the country
(*i*) Competition and other entry wages
(*j*) Success and failure factors
(*k*) Evaluation of venture ideas
(*l*) Planning the business
(*m*) New product/service
(*n*) New technology/productive methods
(*o*) Human resource management
(*p*) Organisation and individual issues
(*q*) Women entrepreneurs
(*r*) Family business
(*s*) International business
(*t*) Financing entrepreneurial ventures
(*u*) Current issues pertaining to entrepreneurship

The methods of imparting education included:

1. Formal lectures in class-room situation.
2. Group exercises by the participants.
3. Presentation of a business plan by each student.
4. Tutorials.

5. A case study of a business unit to be presented in the form of a project report.

These courses were being taught as subsidiary subjects of management and technology, spreading over the period of primary course span.

An indepth enquiry into the design of these programmes creates doubt about their capabilities they claim for obvious reasons:

1. Entrepreneurial characteristics, in general, are innate to the individual, as such, they cannot be cultivated in human personal in a shorter span of time without undergoing experiential processes.
2. Entrepreneurs cannot be grown in education factories of uniform methods and procedures because each entrepreneur is a unique individual who sprouts entrepreneurial activities in unique environmental settings, created by himself. This uniqueness gives the entrepreneur a competitive edge over others, thereby helping them to smoothly navigate their business activities in highly competitive business environment. Uniformity in the developmental efforts for entrepreneurs is not justified. Virtually, all educational effort make sense for entrepreneurial development only when they force the entrepreneurs for self learning and self experience. Thus, these programmes should be geared up for the individual differences of entrepreneurs, which is not possible in the formal settings of institutions.

Nevertheless, a role of these institutions, in helping entrepreneurs should not be undermined. They have potential to contribute. All that, however, needed is to correctly perceive their identity and role in the process of national entrepreneurial resource building. Like financial and other support institutions they should also conceive of themselves as a information support system. Instead of trying to profess the theories and practices of management for indoctrination into the mind of novice business aspirants, they should support them with the information they really need. Instead of telling the entrepreneurs to develop, the institutes should develop themselves in respect of the experienced faculties, entrepreneur identification capabilities and information storage and retrieval flexibilities for meeting the demand of the entrepreneurs quickly. The entrepreneurs are inherently educated and developed in their rich traits which others cannot ordinarily imbibe even in life time. The prime objective of these institutions should be to identify the entrepreneurial resource and induce and support them to harness their potential for good of the national economy.

# 15

# Women Entrepreneurs in Pondicherry: Their Problems and Prospects

—*Dr. P. Palanichamy*

## Introduction

An International Labour Organisation's report in 1980 stated that women are 50 per cent of the world population, do the 2/3 of the worlds work hours, receive 10 per cent of worlds income and own less than 1 per cent of world property. All because of an accident of birth. With regard to India, women constitute 60 per cent of the rural unemployed, and 56 per cent of the total unemployed. If the qualified women entering employment market is calculated, the figure would be more.

This is the position observed in the world as well as at the national level.

With regard to Pondicherry the total women constitute 55 per cent, employed women occupy 49 per cent. Men and women enter organisations equipped with different skill sets. Women have been taught to depend on others, to limit their time perspective and to avoid exposure to risk. As a result of this dependency and other directedness emphasised in female role prescriptions, women become forced to be in the psychological barrier of lack of confidence in self, made incapable of setting goals, to plan or prepare to achieve.

The India Investment Centre, New Delhi in its study about

people of Pondicherry has found that the people of Pondicherry are not industrious, they are risk aversive and hence do not start industries.

The industrial backwardness of Pondicherry up to 1954 (till it was annexed to India) and its systematic growth thereafter may prove this point.

**Table 15.1**
**Comparative Industrial Position of Pondicherry**

| *Up to 1954* | *No. of Units* | *Investment (Rs. in Crores)* | *Employment (No.)* | *Value of Production (Rs. in Crores)* |
|---|---|---|---|---|
| LSS | 3 | N.A. | N.A. | N.A. |
| MSS | NIL | NIL | NIL | NIL |
| SSI | 5 | N.A. | 8000 | N.A. |
| AS ON 31.03.78 | | | | |
| LSS | 27 | 57804 | 14597 | 864.17 |
| MSS | 93 | 217 | 6305 | 668 |
| SSI | 5726 | 160 | 46164 | 1749 |

*Source:* Directorate of Industries and Commerce, Pondicherry.

## Growing Awareness in India

Having realised the importance of the role to be played by women in the nations development, in the Seventh Five Year Plan a chapter on women development has been included and it details the plan of action for "Integration of women in development". The National Convention of Women Entrepreneurs held at New Delhi (1981) called for priority to women in the allotment of land, shed, sanction of power and industrial licencing. The new industrial policy of Government of India also has specifically highlighted the need for conducting special entrepreneurship programmes for women, which would be in the nature of product/process oriented courses to enable them to start small scale industries. It further adds that the objective of this course is to give representation to women in the field of small industry development with a view to uplift their status in the economic and social fields.

Recent researches conduced indicate that several women are now willing to become entrepreneurs due to various factors. These can be divided into two parts, namely, "Pull Factors" and "Push factors".

*Pull Factors:* Under this category women entrepreneurs choose a profession as a challenge and adventure with an urge to do something, new liking for business and to have independent occupation.

*Push Factors:* This category of women takes up business enterprises to get over financial difficulties and responsibilities thrust on them due to family circumstances.

**Scope and Objective of This Study**

This piece of work was basically aimed at analysing as to whether the women entrepreneurship in Pondicherry is as per the trends in India or in any way better or worse than in other places.

**Methodology**

The data was collected through interviews and discussions with the officials of the District Industries Centre, Directorate of Industries and Commerce and the Association of the Small Scale Entrepreneurs of the Union Territory of Pondicherry (ASIUTOP).

The interview conducted with the Secretary of ASIUTOP revealed that there is only a handful of women entrepreneurs who have registered their names with the Association and are actively engaged in running the small scale industrial units.

As per the data provided by the Directorate of Industries and Commerce the growth of the women entrepreneurs in Pondicherry is shown in Table 15.2.

Interviews conducted with the officials of the Directorate of Industries and Commerce revealed that these entrepreneurs were mostly trained by the District Industries Centre, Pondicherry in the Handicrafts section. The interviews and discussions held with the officials of the District Industries Centre, Pondicherry revealed that all the EDPs on handicrafts conducted were only for training women enterpreneurs and therefore these contributed to the growth of women entrepreneurs.

**Table 15.2**
**Growth of Women Entrepreneurs in Pondicherry**

| *Years* | *No. of Women Entrepreneurs* |
|---|---|
| *Up to* 1983-84 | **156** |
| 1984-85 | — |
| 1985-86 | 11 |
| 1986-87 | 31 |
| 1987-88 | 43 |
| 1988-89 | 51 |
| 1989-90 | 44 |
| 1990-91 | 45 |
| 1991-92 | 58 |
| 1992-93 | 72 |
| 1993-94 | 40 |
| 1994-95 | 49 |
| 1995-96 | 52 |
| 1996-97 | 12 |
| 1997-98 | 53 |
| Total | 561 |
| Average | 40 |

*Source:* Directorate of Industries and Commerce, Pondicherry.

## Period of Study

The total number of women enterprises set up in these 14 years of study period are 561 and on a average 40 per year. Another attempt is made to find out the share of the women entrepreneurs in Pondicherry. The share of women entrepreneurs in the industrial growth of Pondhicherry is given in Table 15.3.

The analysis of Table 15.3 reveals that women entrepreneurs constitute only a small percentage of the total SSI units. They were ranging from 4.5 per cent of the total SSI units (1985-86) to 22.6 per cent of the same in the year 1997-98. On an average they were 18.26 per cent of the total SSI units.

**Table 15.3**
**Share of Women Entrepreneurs in Total SSI of Pondicherry**

| *Years* | *Women Entrepreneurs* | *SSIs* | *% Share* |
|---|---|---|---|
| *Up to* 1983-84 | 156 | 1946 | 8 |
| 1984-85 | — | 202 | — |
| 1985-86 | 11 | 244 | 4.5 |
| 1986-87 | 31 | 261 | 11.9 |
| 1987-88 | 43 | 298 | 14.4 |
| 1988-89 | 51 | 358 | 14.2 |
| 1989-90 | 44 | 277 | 15.9 |
| 1990-91 | 45 | 297 | 15.2 |
| 1991-92 | 58 | 356 | 16.3 |
| 1992-93 | 72 | 324 | 22.2 |
| 1993-94 | 40 | 272 | 14.7 |
| 1994-95 | 49 | 301 | 16.3 |
| 1995-96 | 52 | 264 | 19.7 |
| 1996-97 | 12 | 92 | 13.0 |
| 1997-98 | 53 | 234 | 22.6 |
| Total | 561 | 5726 | |
| Average of 14 years | 40 | 270 | 18.26 |

*Source:* Compiled from the data collected from the Directorate of Industries and Commerce.

### Causes for Poor Share of Women Entrepreneurs (Problems)

For the purpose of finding out the reasons for the poor share of the women entrepreneurs an attempt was made to consult the Directorate of Industries and Commerce, District Industries Centre and the Secretary ASIUTOP.

The Information available from the District Industries Centre revealed that except for training, in handicrafts, for no other training programmes, did woman come forward. It was further revealed that no woman came forward for doing any business especially setting up of Industry, either medium or large scale. The SSI units set up by women entrepreneurs are also only handicraft units. Therefore the women entrepreneurs trained by the DIC in handicrafts are the only real women entrepreneurs in Pondicherry.

However, the replies available from the ASIUTOP revealed, that earlier, the fire services department was the thorn in the flesh and it was sought to be removed by the "single window scheme" for quick clearance.

But now the departments, which are the stumbling blocks to the growth of the SSI units in general and women entrepreneurs in particular, are (1) the "Town and Country Planning" department in the rural areas and (2) "Pollution Control Board" in the urban areas and (3) the "Science and Technology Department".

Though the Government of India's directive gives automatic clearance from pollution control department (except for 17 most polluting industries) for starting SSI units just on the submission of the application, the department of Science and Technology, Government of Pondicherry pokes its nose into all these industries, even those like computer and electronics and subjects them to environment/pollution control law.

Similarly, the Town and Country Planning department rejects domestic industries like gem cutting, data processing, etc., in the residential areas, even when they are started by the women entrepreneurs directing them to go to industrial estates (far away from residential areas).

Sometimes being a woman itself is a hurdle for becoming an entrepreneur. Women are not able to go here and there freely and mobilise funds, raw materials, or market their products as their male counterparts. Society expects her to be a home loving affectionate lady. Family members expects her to do any business without a challenge for her status as a woman. Customers, clients, etc., give a differential treatment to a woman than given to a male entrepreneur. As a result, in spite of the ambitions, education, enlightenment, they are made to go in for any jobs like a Doctor, Engineer, Advocate, Executive, etc., but are not facilitated to be entrepreneurs especially in Pondicherry. This is in spite of the fact that it is a "City State".

The extreme comment from the ASIUTOP is that the schemes for women entrepreneurs are only on paper and not implemented in practice.

**Prospects for the Women Entrepreneurs**

The new industrial policy formulated by the government of Pondicherry states that the "Women entrepreneurs would be motivated through training and orientation programme. Women with special aptitude, skills and capability would be identified for development of entrepreneurship among them. Ten per cent of the plots and sheds in the industrial estates will be reserved for women entrepreneurs." (Highlights of the Industrial Policy 1997 — Government of Pondicherry, p. 5).

The Pondicherry Industrial Promotion Development and Investment Corporation (PIPDIC) has evolved a new scheme for women entrepreneurs, namely, Mahila Udhyama Nidhi for helping them to set up new projects in tiny/small scale sector.

Single Window Scheme has been implemented in the DIC campus for the purpose of facilitating entrepreneurs to set up new projects in SSI/Tiny sector, new promotees for acquiring fixed assets and for existing entrepreneurs when they go in for modernisation and also for rehabilitation of sick industrial units.

ASIUTOP is approaching the Union Finance Minister for directing the commercial banks to adhere to Nayak Committees recommendations, whereby the minimum credit limit sanctioned to SSI units shall be 20 per cent of the projected annual turnover and the maximum margin participation by the SSI units shall be 20 per cent. This may ease out the problem of working capital finance and to that extent it may relieve the women entrepreneurs from the problem of working capital.

ASIUTOP also demands that factoring service for the post-sale bills be directed to be provided by the SIDBI directly through agencies to SSI factor.

RBI is requested to permit for starting separate Industrial Co-operative Banks by the SSI units with capital participation by the SIDBI and State Government.

These are the measures taken for helping the women entrepreneurs at the time of starting an enterprise and financing.

In view of the problems faced by the women entrepreneurs, in establishing and running a business there are certain businesses identified by the government of Pondicherry and other agencies in the new industrial policy 1997 which are best suited for the women entrepreneurs. They are:

1. Agro processing including marine products.
2. Electronics and Software developments.
3. Textiles including garments.

The Government of Pondicherry is creating the Export Promotion Cell and Export Processing Zone to promote industrial growth in Pondicherry.

Apart from these, there are some other industries which can be set up and run by women entrepreneurs being at home itself like

*(a)* Computer software services
*(b)* Agarbatti manufacturing
*(c)* Papad making
*(d)* Handicrafts for exports
*(e)* Travel agency services
*(f)* Xeroxing firms
*(g)* Stationery manufacturing units
*(h)* Pickle manufacturing units, etc.

**Promising Future**

A Modern Growth Centre cum Industrial Estate at Polagam in Karaikal (a part of Pondicherry) is being finalised. A Coir Development Industrial Estate and Growth Centre is likely to be established in Ariyankuppam (a suburb of Pondicherry). A Software Technology Park in Pondicherry is proposed. 187 investment proposals are currently in the pipeline promising a total outlay of about Rs. 2042 crores, having potential to employ over 19,894 persons. Several renowned multinational corporations like Tatas, Thapars, TVS, SPIC, Kotharis, Shrirams, L&T, Chemfab, Whirlpool, Ownes-Bilt, Hindustan Lever, Foseco, Ponds, Henkel, Chemcrown, etc., are setting up industries in Pondicherry. As a result of these, there may be a need for the ancillaries and job contractors also, i.e., SSI Units. These may provide for the assured demand for the products and hence under the easy condition of credit, women may come forward for setting up business in Pondicherry.

## Summary

In India women constitute 60 per cent of the rural unemployed and 56 per cent of the total unemployed. Society is changing especially after the conferences of the women entrepreneurs (1981) and some of the EDPs conducted by certain specialist institutions. This has resulted in the growth of women entrepreneurs in Pondicherry also.

There are some inherent problems for the women entrepreneurs, but the steps taken by the Government, Association of Small Scale Entrepreneurs, etc., are likely to convert these problems into a promising future. The infrastructural facilities available in Pondicherry, incentives and subsidies available, emerging large-scale multinational corporations, growth centres, export processing zones, promise good prospects for women entrepreneurs.

## Reference

1. P. Saravanavel, *Entrepreneurial Development Principles, Policies and Programmes*, Ess Pee Kay Publishing House, Chennai, 1991, p. 62.

# 16

# New Dynamics in Entrepreneurship Training Design

—*Dr. N.P. Srinivasan*
—*D. Selvanayakam*

## Introduction

The Entrepreneurship Institute is a non-profit organisation specialising in the development of strategies for creating jobs by assisting entrepreneurs to start businesses or to expand their young firms. The Entrepreneurship Institute programmes assist entrepreneurs by direct involvement and financial support of the leadership of the community within which the programmes are conducted. The Institute organises a directorship of leading bankers, lawyers, accountants, entrepreneurs and other entrepreneurial support resources with which it shares decision making and programme planning responsibility. As a high level network of support with contracts in the entrepreneurial community, this group is asked to assume a leadership role in creating new businesses, helping to expand young firms and providing jobs in the area.

## Evaluation of EDPs

Taking into consideration the fact that the strategy of training potential entrepreneurs through EDPs constitutes an important policy instrument and that substantial amount of funds are annually committed to train potential entrepreneurs, a need is felt to undertake a systematic and comprehensive evaluation of the programmes.

*Firstly,* being a dynamic activity, EDPs should be subjected to continuous renewal and restructuring to meet the ever-changing requirements of the potential entrepreneurs and the policy environment.

*Secondly,* in the context of a developing economy, the use of scarce resources for any developmental activity should be justified in terms of the costs involved and benefits flowing from it.

*Thirdly,* the credibility and sustainability of a developmental activity greatly depends upon the extent to which it achieves its stated objectives.

All this suggests an indepth evaluation and introspection of the ED movement in the country. No doubt, India has made a breakthrough in making entrepreneurial awareness among enterprising people in the last 30 years. Although the situation is much more satisfactory today than what it was when the EDP movement started, the debate about whom to train and what constitutes an effective training package is as fierce as ever before. Perhaps it has become even more so in recent years. Thus, the EDP strategy informing the programmes and the process are still not complete.

The most important input in the implementation process is the trainee. Officials of the support system as also the trainer motivators often refer to the poor quality of the trainees. It is primarily because neither adequate promotional campaign is carried out nor scientifically devised selection tools are used by most organisations to select candidates with good entrepreneurial potential. Very often the organisers are handicapped by poor response to the programmes and accept whosoever is available. Sometimes, the trainers are not equipped to properly administer the selection tools. This would require that the selection capabilities of trainer-motivators are improved. It is also necessary to develop different selection tools keeping in view the specific needs of specific target groups.

In India, as in many other developing economies, enterprise training programmes usually aim at poverty alleviation or income generation and almost totally disregard the social/socio-economic objectives of personal development. There is very little emphasis on training in the area of business skills like opportunity identification, cost estimation, growth planning and the such. The universal applicability of this paradigm has only lately begun to be called into question, as awareness of the link between cultural values and approaches to entrepreneurship has come to be recognized. Even so, most enterprise training programmes depend heavily on Western models and are by and large transferred/adopted from the West with very little thought given to their limitations in an alien context. "Entrepreneurship development is very susceptible to cultural values which impact upon motivation differently in different regions . . . the transfer of experience from one country to another is no easy task and needs to be handled with a great deal of empathy and care. It is imperative that requirements of enterprise training in the Indian context be researched in detail and training programmes and designs be adapted to suit these requirements."

Here are some of the suggestions to the Entrepreneurial Training (ET) designers.

***1. Understanding ET***

We wonder why the word "training" is used both for disciplining so-called dumb animals and for helping intelligent human beings achieve their potential at work. The two activities seem on the face of it so much further apart than do "training" from, say, "education". Why do we call it "training" not "education?" The immediate response is, "Because it's about changing attitude/ behaviour". This seems to us now, on more experienced reflection, to contain more than a grain of truth. Usually what organisations and individuals are looking for from the ET activities is a demonstrable change in behaviour. So here is the first key point about the nature of entrepreneurial training. At its root, it is about changing people's behaviour. There are a few other key characteristics of entrepreneurial training that the ET designers need to recognise at the outset. Again, they can be identified in contrast with general education.

- Acquisition of knowledge (K) does not necessarily lead to behavioural change.
- Acquisition of skill (S) also may not lead to change in behaviour.
- Changes in attitude (A) would normally lead towards behavioural change.

- The ET designers, therefore, must aim at bringing out changes in the outlook of the person. Change in the attitude and outlook towards particular job he is engaged in, would direct him automatically to acquire more knowledge and skill. (But let us not get the impression that every training brings out behavioural change.)

| *Education/Teaching* | *Training* |
|---|---|
| * Predominantly for children and youth | * Predominantly for adults |
| * General Objectives, e.g. to learn French | * Focussed objectives, e.g., to learn how to conduct an interview. |
| * "Normal", i.e., often what everyone in a particular age group is doing. | * "Special", i.e., time is taken off "normal" work activities to do it. |
| * Emphasis is on knowledge transfer. | * Emphasis is on behaviour change. |
| * Little to do with job improvement | * Caters to job improvement. |
| * Learning from the work experience of teacher | * Learning through work experience of group |
| * Teacher centred approach | * Group centred approach. |

### 2. Conceptual Framework of ET Design

The ET design could be viewed as an enterprise building activity and on the other as a human resource development strategy. Albeit, both the approaches are geared towards creating an overall environment where entrepreneurship germinates and grows. The first approach is converting a potential entrepreneur into an actual entrepreneur, the assumption being that the ET intervention can bridge the gap between those who are born in a business family and those who lack the advantages of such an immediate environment. The other view looks at EDPs as a human resource development activity. It holds that the contribution of EDPs goes much beyond enterprise creation. One of the critical objectives of EDPs is to inculcate entrepreneurial values in a society where environment for natural supply of entrepreneurs may not be very conducive and to widen the base of entrepreneurial supply by bringing such potential entrepreneurs into the fold of entrepreneurship through the ET intervention. Whatever the approach taken, the ET designer would see to it, the programmes would suit the participants taking into account the immediate environment of the participants.

### 3. *ET Pay-offs*

To understand the challenges and opportunities of training and to design entrepreneurial training in a way that meets the former and exploits the latter, the ET designers must be explicit about the pay-offs the organisation is expecting.

*The Skills Pay-off*

The ET designers invest in training to produce a more skilled entrepreneur. In the vast majority of cases, the ET designers specify quite precisely the skills for the trainees to acquire in order to better meet the requirements and challenges of future enterprises. Such training is typically focussed on those trainees who need particular skills.

*The Cultural Pay-off*

The ET designers invest in training to change the way things are done around here. It is to bring about greater awareness of the things of the old culture and to go beyond its boundary in new culture. Participants feel inspired to reach the goal and this leads to increased vitality. They are prepared to work hard and achieve visible results. This in turn reinforces their values. Thus healthy culture is based on encouragement, enterprise and excellence.

*The Morale Pay-off*

Providing access to high quality entrepreneurial training is seen as a mark of efficient ET designers. It is evident that the ET designers value the trainees. So the ET designers offer training provision to the trainees not only before venturing into business but also after commencing business. This is called ongoing formation/training. This is done with a view to keep them happy with their firms, to raise their level of energy in the enterprising activities and to make them feel that ET designers made a significant and worthwhile investment in them.

Of course, many ET programmes are looking for multiple pay offs in skills, culture and morale. An ET programme, for example, is intended to give aspiring entrepreneurs new techniques for problem-solving (skills), encourage flexible and adjusting patterns from rigidity (culture), and raise energy level after a round of compulsory redundancies (morale).

### 4. *First Things First*

Since life is busy and full of change, keeping "first things first" is a constant challenge. Maintaining focus and regaining vision is a constant need. Because the ET is primarily about behaviour change and not knowledge transfer, the ET designer needs to be most concerned with the learners and much less concerned with what is to be learned. People often go into education out of an enthusiasm for their subject and often the E T designers are much more likely to be motivated by enthusiasm for people. The classic mistake in the ET design is to be seduced by the logic and beauty of the training content, forgetting until later the participants who will receive the training. The training frame which the ET designers introduce is one way of ensuring that in their approach to training design they put people first. If the ET design is the science of putting first things first, then the ET becomes the art of putting first things first. The greatest resource in any ET design is the group. If the ET deliverer taps into that resource, the group will do half of the work for him before the group even enters the training spot. This is the process of imagining that group as it approaches the training and of tapping into their feelings, values and concerns.

### 5. *Key Dimensions of ET Design*

The ET has to prove its relevance, because on the whole it is part of the work. And the reason why training has little effect on behaviour at work is that, quite simply, the participants don't believe in it. So the ET designers must ask themselves at every stage: What can I do to increase the credibility of this ET intervention? Otherwise their training will meet with cynical rejection.

*Commitment*

It is about investment. The more each participant invests

personally in a programme, the more effect it will have. At the same time the ET designers must look for opportunities throughout the intervention to gain more commitment from the participants. Unless the ET designers elicit significant commitment from each participant, there is a risk that they will sit back and mentally say, "This is all well and good. But basically it's for somebody else."

*Risk*

To get commitment, the ET designers/deliverers have to set people to take risks. They must make sure the degree of risk they expect their participants to take is proportional to the degree of benefit they can expect to get in return and appropriate to their emotional state. The ET designers should not expect the participants to take high risks at the start of a programme. One good relationship is built up among them, the ET designers could ask them to take risk gradually in the group by way of giving feedback, coaching one another and discussing differences. At the same time, if the ET designers draft no/low risk ET programmes, no/low impact will be the result. If they throw high risk interventions at people with no lead-in, or lead-out, participants will, quite simply, walk away from the training.

*Attention*

Participants level of attention fluctuates. It declines when people are passive/listening/watching without action/bored. It declines when they know what is coming is not interesting. The ET designers need to approach their task as a fight against the decline of attention.

*Manoeuvrability*

The E T designers and deliverers are a partnership, even when they don't know each other. Of course, they are often one and the same, and that is ideal. But even when they are not, the success of an intervention depends on both their efforts, and it depends at least as much on the deliverer's skill-in-making the training work as it does on the designer's skill in putting it together in the first place. The training deliverer needs to be allowed the space and opportunity to adapt the programme to the group, to the atmosphere, to events which occur unexpectedly in and outside the training room. The course needs to be designed for manoeuvrability.

***6. Weighing Up the Training Challengers: The "Training Frame"***

The size of the challenge in any particular piece of training design will depend on the balance of forces working for and forces working against. Now the ET designers shall look at a way of positioning a training intervention which will alert you to the forces operating for and against that specific intervention. The frame comprises three dimensions.

**The Training Frame**

| | |
|---|---|
| Job Specific | General |
| Chosen | Imposed |
| Head based | Heart based |

*'Job Specific' Vs 'General'*

This dimension is about the nature of the behaviour change the ET designer is required to deliver. At one end of the spectrum is behaviour change highly specific to the participant's job. An example would be training for recruiting managers in the use of a personality questionnaire. They are not required to use the knowledge and skills acquired for anything other than their job. At the other end of the spectrum is behaviour change affecting the whole of the participant's life. An example would be training in 'interpersonal skills' courses.

*'Chosen Change' Vs 'Imposed Change '*

This dimension is pretty self-explanatory. An example of chosen change would be when participants decide they want to improve their competence in budgeting and apply to go on a financial management course. An example of imposed change would be if managers sent them.

*'Head Based' Vs. 'Heart Based'*

When an ET intervention is only about imparting knowledge, it is totally head based. An example would be a module in an induction programme on organisational structure. When an ET intervention is only about changing attitudes, it is totally heart based. Examples would be a training programme to sell a new set of 'values' to employees.

### *7. Mixed Personality Classes*

It is more important for the ET designers to have some framework for understanding individual differences in learning than to use any particular one. For any framework will guide you to the key fact that a training intervention must engage in a variety of ways, at a range of levels, if it is to engage a group of participants.

How people learn: A framework of the most important differences

| | | |
|---|---|---|
| Extrovert | as opposed to | Introvert |
| Evidence-seeking | as opposed to | Concept-loving |
| Logic-led | as opposed to | Values driven |
| Structured | as opposed to | Fluid |

*'Extrovert' Vs 'Introvert' Learners*

Extrovert learners try new experiment/skill and learn through action. They learn with others through interaction. They learn things which make a difference and get bored by spending too much time learning on their own. Introvert learners reflect on new experiment/skill and need encouragement to gain a degree of mastery. They learn things privately but surprise others by their individualistic insights/inner life after a long silence. but they get cumulative stressed by a high quantity of action and interaction. So the ET designers can arrange inputs on the different elements of personal development to the whole group (Career development workshop). In those sessions, participants could choose whether to listen quietly or participate in discussion or exploration of their own case. Each input is followed by a session in which the participants could choose whether to join a group or to work alone or in pairs.

*'Evidence-seeking' Vs. 'Concept-loving' Learners*

Evidence-seekers like to see the step by step logic behind what they are learning. They like to know about the evidence behind a new approach: they will typically ask questions such as 'where' and 'how'. They are unimpressed by theory. Concept-loving learners like patters/concepts/theory. They are interested in future possibilities/changes. They give a new approach to experiment/innovate things. They are true innovators and enthusiasts for development. For these people, the ET designers should have design training in layers. There will be parts of any training programme to which everyone is exposed, such as the tutor's presentations to the whole group. But there are other parts which some of the participants may not even be aware of, unless they need to be. So the ET designers can visualise a piece of training design as a stack of layers: participants choose how deep they go.

*'Logic-led' Vs. 'Values-driven' Learners*

Some people learn more with their heads (logic-led), others more with their hearts (values-driven). Logic led learners are detached, concerned about task accomplishment, tough-minded and focussed on analytical rigour. Values-driven learners are emotionally bound up with their learning, concerned about people's feelings and challenging of the values behind training. What the existence of these two perspectives on learning means for the ET designers is that both the intellectual credibility of the training and also its ethical credibility must be established.

*Structured Vs. 'Fluid' Learners*

Structured learners like to know where they are going, get there and then know where they have been. When it comes to sign-posting, they need even more of it than the average participant. They like training with regular structure, very clearly stated objectives, specific action-planning sessions, practical check lists and a definite end. Fluid learners are less demanding in ways. They are picking things up opportunistically, enjoying a certain amount of chaos and spontaneity. They rather enjoy changes to the programme and they are prepared to embark on an activity without always knowing what it is intended to achieve. Of all the dimensions, this one is the most difficult to design successfully for both ends of the best combination of learning preferences in each group they deliver. That way, the deliverers can respond to the particular combination of learning preferences in each group they deliver the training to.

**Conclusion**

What the ET designers need to exploit this potential for their own development as a training designer is feedback. They need to deliver at least some of the training they design, sit it on courses they have designed which are delivered by someone else, talk of deliverers, participants and customers. They must ask:

- What worked well ?
- What could have been different and worked better ?

There is no perfect training intervention, thank goodness, because the variability, in genuity and unpredictability of people can never be totally accounted for. So they must make it a habit to criticise the training they have designed, to identify its weak points and to spot the places it fails to engage. If they do this, they will design as ET that is good enough. The trainer-motivators are the backbone of an EDP, who can make or mar its performance. It is necessary for an ED organisation to have a well qualified, competent and committed cadre of trainer-motivators.

**References**

1. Awasthi Dinesh N. and Sebastian Jose (1996), *Evaluation of Entrepreneurship Development Programmes*, Saha Publications, New Delhi.
2. Covery, Stephen R. (1997), *First Things First*, A Fireside Book, New York.
3. Fayyaz Ahmed (1998), *Vocationalisation of Business Education*, Vol. 4 (1 & 2).
4. Hardingham Alison (1997), *Designing Training*, Universities Press, Hyderabad.
5. Harbar Dean and Ciparis Ramona (1990), "*Youth Action Guide on Sustainable Development*," Shell International & Co. Ltd., London.
6. Naagendra, P. (1985), *Entrepreneurship Development*, Inter-cultural Foundation for Development, New Delhi.
7. Nayak, A.K. (1997), *Guidance and Counselling*, APH Publishing Corporation, New Delhi.
8. Pegg Mike (1998), *Positive Leadership*, UBSPD, New Delhi.
9. Ravindra Kothavade (1994), *Indian Entrepreneurship*, EDI Publications, Ahmedabad.
10. Sunanda Easwaran (1994), *Indian Entrepreneurship*, EDI Publications, Ahmedabad.
11. Venkatapathy and Rajamohan (1994), *Entrepreneurship Awareness*, EDI Publications, Ahmedabad.

# 17

# Role of District Industries Centre in Entrepreneurial Development in Manipur

—*Dr. G.P. Prasain*
—*Prof. N. C. Das*

## Introduction

Entrepreneurial development is essentially an educational process and an endeavour in human resource development. Entrepreneurs are not just born, they can be developed and framed to undertake ventures and be creative. However, everybody does not have the potential to become an entrepreneur. It requires an environment in which an entrepreneur can learn and discharge his functions. Stepanch identifies intelligence, motivation, knowledge and opportunity as the prerequisites for entrepreneurial development. First of all the entrepreneurs must be endowed with above average intelligence. Motivation is not inherited but a personal and cultural trait. Knowledge can be acquired through formal education and experience. Entrepreneurs can overcome many obstacles of development, and if given sufficient time, can create opportunity.

Entrepreneurship Development incorporate four basic issues, viz.,

*(i)* the availability of material resources,
*(ii)* the solution of real entrepreneurs,

(*iii*) the formation of industrial units, and
(*iv*) policy formulation for the development of the region.

All these issues are closely inter-related.

An entrepreneurial development programme (EDP) is based on the belief that individuals can be converted into action through an organised and systematic programme. EDP is not merely a training programme. It is a process of

(*a*) enhancing the motivation, knowledge and skills of the potential entrepreneurs,
(*b*) arousing and reforming the entrepreneurial behaviour in their day to day activities,
(*c*) assisting them develop their own ventures or enterprises as a sequel to entrepreneurial action.

Prof. Hosclitz also suggests that entrepreneurship can develop in a society where its culture permits a variety of choices and where social processes are not rigid and in a situation which encourages the development of personalities interested in enterprise.

**Manipur: Its Industrial Scenario**

Manipur is a land-locked state situated in the extreme corner of North-Eastern India. This state is rectangular in shape, with a mountainous terrain. The highest mountain is 3000 metres above the mean sea level. It lies within the latitude of 23.83" N and 25.69" N and longitude 93.03" E and 94.74" E. The total geographical area of Manipur is 22.327 Sq. km. It has two distinct areas of hills and plains. The area of plains or valley which is located in the centre of Manipur is only 1,862 Sq. km. There are 8 (eight) districts in Manipur. Out of which 3 (three) districts are in the valley and rest 5 (five) districts are situated in the sprawling hills. Manipur occupies 0.68 per cent and 8.75 per cent of the area of the whole country and the entire North-Eastern Region respectively.

Manipur is still industrially very backward even in the backward N.E. Region of India with per capita income far below the all India average, viz., Rs. 3502 at current prices at the end of the Seventh Plan Period in 1989-90 as against the all India average of Rs. 4252.50. As many as 45.06 per cent of the people of the State live below the poverty line in 1992-93 as against the all India average of 25 per cent by the end of the Seventh Plan and 18 per cent now. There are not enough industries to keep pace with the rapid growth of population and to deal with the growing problems of unemployment, poverty, lack of housing and medical care, etc. Added to this, there is the problem of comparative neglect of industrialisation in the State Planning. For instance, the 6th plan allocation for the industrial sector in Manipur was 8.33 per cent as against the all India average of 12.28 per cent.

There are hardly any major or medium industrial units in the state worth the name and the few that have already been established are now suffering from varying degrees of industrial sickness. Development of large scale industries has to follow its own logic and such major industrial units cannot be established anywhere. But that is not so in the case of small scale and household industries. Given the proper policies and programmes and reasonably adequate infra-structural support, there are no small scale and household industries either demand based or resource based, which cannot be successfully established in Manipur.

There are two types of small industrial units in Manipur, viz., SIDO (Small Industries Development Organisation) and non-SIDO. In the SIDO group, there are Small Service Establishment (SSE) units which are Colour Photography, X-ray, Xeroxing, Automobile Workshops, etc., and Manipur Small Industries (MSI) units producing goods which are not in the reserved items such as wool knitting, embriodery, blacksmithy, carpentry, handicraft items, etc. Total number of registered SIDO and non-SIDO units, employment, investment and production in all the eight districts of Manipur up to 1994-95 are shown in Table 17.1.

Table 17.1 reveals that up to the year 1994-95, the total number of permanently registered units in the SIDO group were 5351 and 2990 in the non-SIDO group. The total number of permanently registered units in both the SIDO and non-SIDO groups were 8341 with total investment, production and employment of Rs. 27.37 crores, Rs. 123.16 crores and 42720 persons respectively.

### D.I.C. and Entrepreneurship Development Programme

A District Industries Centre (DIC) is an institution at the district level which provides all the services and facilities to

**Table 17.1**

| *District* | *SIDO* | *Non-SIDO* | *Total* | *Employ-ment* | *Invest-ment (Rs. in Crores)* | *Produc-tion (Rs. in Crores)* |
|---|---|---|---|---|---|---|
| 1. Imphal | 2774 | 2161 | 4935 | 25375 | 16.17 | 72.12 |
| 2. Bishnupur | 420 | 160 | 580 | 2516 | 1.90 | 8.35 |
| 3. Thoubal | 305 | 96 | 401 | 2121 | 1.32 | 5.77 |
| 4. Churachand-pur | 429 | 104 | 533 | 2781 | 1.76 | 8.68 |
| 5. Senapati | 251 | 49 | 300 | 1616 | 0.99 | 4.38 |
| 6. Ukhrul | 715 | 88 | 803 | 4134 | 2.62 | 12.56 |
| 7. Tamenglong | 248 | 203 | 451 | 2371 | 1.49 | 6.49 |
| 8. Chandel | 209 | 129 | 338 | 1806 | 1.12 | 4.87 |
| Total | 5351 | 2990 | 8341 | 42720 | 27.37 | 123.16 |

*Sources:* Nucleus Cell, Industries Depat., Govt. of Manipur.

entrepreneurs at one place so that they may set up small and village industries. These services and facilities include the identification of the suitable scheme, the preparation of a feasibility report, arrangements for the supply of machinery and equipment, provision of raw materials, credit facilities and input for marketing and extension services, quality control, research and entrepreneurial training. The District Industries Centre would also ensure that small industries continue to be viable. For this purpose, it provides all the facilities to the entrepreneurs under one roof at the district and sub-district levels.

District Industries Centre's are established in all the eight districts of Manipur and all these DICs are giving different types of training programme to the entrepreneurs because unless entrepreneurs are first developed, there is no question of improving the industries which are bound to play an active role in the growth process of the state economy. Entrepreneurial motivation and training is one of the most important factors which accelerates the pace of industrial development by inducing people to undertake risk bearing activities. The main objective of conducting Entrepreneurship

Development Programmes (EDP) is to motivate the young and promising entrepreneurs for self-employment after successful completion of training. The first batch of EDP in Manipur was taken up in the year 1983-84 under the sponsorship of the State Bank of India providing training to 24 persons including 2 females. Since then, several batches of EDP have been conducted from time to time by the State Directorate of Industries under the auspices of different organisations such as NISIET (National Institute of Small Industries, Extension and Training), NEITCO (North Eastern Industrial Training Consultancy Organisation), SISI (Small Industries Service Institute), etc., and by 1991-92, altogether 997 persons were given training under EDP.

EDP training courses and other entrepreneurial activities conducted by the DICs of Manipur with the help of different consultancy agencies cover EDP training courses, EDP on Science and Technology, EDP for backward classes, Rural EDP, EDP training on food processing, Entrepreneurs and Enterprise Building Programme, Industrial management, Institutional Meet, Financial Management, District Level Seminars, etc.

It is revealed that EDP training courses were started in DICs of Maipur from 1985-86 and DIC Imphal is the first DIC in Manipur where one and three EDP training courses were started with participation of 25 and 60 people during the year 1985-86 and 1986-87 respectively. During 1987-88 all the DICs of Manipur except DIC Churachandpur conducted EDP training courses. In the year 1988-89 DIC Churachandpur also conducted one EDP training course with 25 participants. Maximum number of EDP training courses were conducted in different DICs of Manipur during the year 1987-88 followed by 1993-94, 1994-95, 1992-93, 1988-89, 1990-91 and 1995-96. It also reveals that the maximum number of people participated in the training programme during the year 1993-94 followed by 1987-88, 1992-93, 1994-95, 1988-89, 1990-91 and 1995-96 respectively. All the DICs of Manipur are giving much importance on EDP programme and every year they are conducting many programmes for the benefit of entrepreneurs. The total number of training programmes so far conducted by all the eight DICs of Manipur till the year 1995-96 are 59 and total number of people who have participated in the training programmes are 1540. Among the different DIC of Manipur, DIC Imphal conducted the maximum numbers of EDP training courses with maximum numbers of participants during this period.

The trained entrepreneurs are provided with different incentives/facilities by the State government to help them in the development process. In terms of the Industrial Policy, the incentives are 15:

1. Allotment of land except to the village and household industries.
2. Allotment of sheds to SSI Units.
3. Manpower Development.
4. State Capital investment subsidy to the priority sector.
5. State transport subsidy for transportation of raw materials and finished products.
6. Interest subsidy.
7. Power subsidy.
8. Subsidy or drawal of power line.
9. Subsidy for feasibility study and project report preparation.
10. Subsidy for technical know how.
11. Price preference.
12. Reimbursement and exemption of local sales tax.
13. Reimbursement of stamp duty and registration fee.
14. Quality control subsidy, and
15. Rehabilitation of viable sick industrial units.

With the introduction of the DIC programme, all the programmes of erstwhile RIP (Rural Industries Project) and RAP (Rural Artisan Project) are implemented through the DICs besides SSI, handloom and handicrafts and Khadi and Village Industries Programmes. The following facilities and incentives are made available to the entrepreneurs and artisans through the DICs.

1. Registration of industrial units quickly and liberally.
2. Credit facilities from banks and other financial institutions for the bankable schemes.
3. Assistance to procure raw materials from Manipur Industrial Development Corporation and other sources.
4. Arrangements for marketing of finished products of registered industrial units.

5. Arrangement for imparting training to rural artisans as well as entrepreneurs.
6. Purchase of machinery on hire purchase basis.
7. Extension service such as providing techno-economic survey reports, area survey reports, reports of prospective industries, reports of industrial project profiles, etc.
8. Follow up programme for ex-trainee for self employment.
9. Infrastructural facilities including allotment of shades of the industrial Estate, power connection, water connection etc.

**Conclusion and Suggestions**

As we are all aware the main thrust of EDP training is not only to strengthen the entrepreneurial traits of the participating trainees but also to help them to launch and manage their ventures successfully. Such training might turn out to be an exercise in futility if the following (feed-back) is weak and is not taken seriously. In order to strengthen the feedback activities after completion of the EDP training courses, back the General Managers, DICs should take necessary measures by entrusting the EDP scheme exclusively to one responsible officer not below the rank of Financial Manager, DIC.

The Selection Committee should take special care for selection of genuine and interested trainees based on their technical backgrounds in any trade, their interest for becoming an entrepreneur, as well as financial backgrounds of their parents. The involvement of the bank representatives should be a must.

The participating trainees select any business/project at random without having any room for consideration about the merits and demerits of their business/project in details. The failure and success of any venture solely depends upon the scheme/project he/she chooses. At this stage, the EDP trainer-motivator, who is the overall in-charge of the EDP, should guide the trainees in the proper and appropriate ways while selecting the business/scheme/project by the trainees keeping in mind the priority sector, non-priority sector and negative sector as per guidelines of the State government and Government of India and advise them to choose demand-based projects with easily available raw materials.

The final objective of an Entrepreneur is to start his/her

venture with financial support from commercial banks and financial institutions. But there is a hurdle on the way to banks/ financial institutions. The loan applications submitted to the banks by an Entrepreneur for credit facilities are not entertained by the banks financial institutions and are found lying in the banks unattended to, without giving any reason and attitude of the bank personals towards the entrepreneurs are not encouraging. Further, banks are in a habit of not releasing even already sanctioned loan cases on the ground of poor recovery of previous loan cases among other things.

The prevailing rigidition of the banks financial procedure should be relaxed to some reasonable extent so as to get the banks financial help in the case of feasible and viable schemes to be launched by promising and new entrepreneurs. Short duration training on Extension Motivation Programme should also be imparted to the bank personal from time to time. And as for loan recovery is concerned, a joint effort may also be made with active participation of bank personals and DIC field staff.

## Reference

1. Joseph, E. Stepanch, *Managers for Small Industries – An International Study*, Asia Publishing House, Bombay, 1962, p. 7.
2. Gupta, C.B., Srinivasan, N.P., *Entrepreneurial Development*, Sultan Chand and Sons, New Delhi, 1996, pp. 4-19.
3. Singh, N.P., *Emerging Trends in Entrepreneurship Development – Theory and Practice*, IFDM, New Delhi, 1985.
4. Hoselitz, B.F., *Sociological Aspects of Economic Growth*, Feffer and Simon Pvt. Ltd., Bombay, 1960, pp. 64-65.
5. Government of Manipur, *Annual Plan, 1993-94*, p. 6
6. *Ibid.*, p. 6.
7. Singh, H.N., *Review of Plans, Policies and Incenties of Government and their Impact*, Paper presented in the Seminar on Dynamics of Entrepreneurship Development in Manipur (unpublished_, p. 1.
8. *Background Note for State Planning Board Meeting*, Manipur, held on 17-11-93.
9. Singh, H.N., *op.cit.*, p. 2
10. *Ibid.*
11. Desai, Vasant, *Organisation and Management of Small Scale Industries*, Himalaya Publishing House, Bombay, 1983, p. 110.
12. Government of Manipur, *EDP* section.
13. Government of Manipur, *Industrial Policy, 1990 and 1995*, Part-III.
14. Government of Manipur, DICs, *Performance and Achievements Report of DIC (Imphal)*, 1992, p. 4.

# 18

# Role of Entrepreneurship in Economic Development

—*Prof. J.V. Prabhakara Rao*
—*Dr. V.K. Bhaskara Rao*

## Entrepreneurship

Entrepreneurship of conceptualised entity, is a useful and innovative strategy for economic development in any country. Entrepreneurs are a special group of persons who enjoy a distinct status and play a crucial role in the success of any business and trade. Economic growth of a nation draws vital initiative from a stream of young and talented entrepreneurs. These are the people having initiative, enterprising ability, zeal and imagination to break through the traditional barriers of commerce and industry, who can translate any business proposal into prospective reality. In the words of Joseph A. Schumpeter, "The entrepreneur in an advanced economy is an individual who introduces something new in the economy—a method of production not yet tested by experience in the branch of manufacture concerned; a product with which consumers are not yet familiar, a new source of raw material or of new markets and the like." Among the economists, Schumpter was the first to identify the importance of entrepreneurship in his theory of economic development. Basically, an entrepreneur is one who assumes risks and uncertainties, seizes opportunities for economic gain, initiates activity leading to production through interaction of men and materials by performing the managerial functions of decision making.

## Entrepreneurship and Economic Development

In the economic development of a country, the human factor plays an important role. Even the developed nations like USA, UK, and Japan have realised the need to promote entrepreneurship for their economic development. These countries could transform their small agro-based industries into big industrial giants only with the support of entrepreneurial abilities. The advent of industrial era in most of the countries, including India, has led to an unprecedented growth of corporate enterprises. Practically speaking, financial, physical and infrastructural facilities are the crucial inputs in the progress of entrepreneurship. There has been widespread growth of realisation of entrepreneurship in the post-independent India. Entrepreneurship would enable all the resources of economy to be used to the maximum extent resulting in significant development.

## Government Initiatives

Of late, industrial enterprises in India are operating under great pressure and in severe competitive environment. Many industries are facing problems like scarcity of capital, low availability of power, low return on investment, limited market outlets and labour problem, etc. The problems of this type would cause increasing risks and uncertainties in trade and industry. While the infrastructural facilities for development and entrepreneurial skills in India are inadequate, the promotional role of the government assumes special significance at a time when high priority and heavy investment industries are given due emphasis. The efforts are being made by Government agencies and institutions to undertake the task of entrepreneurial development.

The government has initiated policies to develop and promote industrial, self-employment. The major schemes like TRYSEM, SEEYU, Prime Minister's Rozgar Yojana (PMRY), etc., have been introduced by the Government to promote self-employment opportunities. These programmes have proved to be the most beneficial for our people. The government has set up a number of institutions with the objective of developing entrepreneurship specifically to improve small business and for promoting avenues for self-employment. A few development banks set-up Entrepreneurship Development Institute of India (EDDI) at Ahmedabad in 1983 to serve as a national resource organisation to facilitate and guide the state level agencies like State Technical Consultancy Organisations (16), Small Industry Service Institutes (16) and nationalised banks. Another All India Institute which came into existence for serving this objective is National Institute of Entrepreneurship and Small Business Development (NIESBD) at New Delhi and this was set up by the Ministry of Industry, Government of India.

It may be noted that development banks and commercial banks have also taken initiative to sponsor entrepreneurship development training programmes. The Industrial Development Bank of India (IDBI) and State Bank of India (SBI) are perhaps the two major institutions which took a lead two decades ago to sponsor entrepreneurial training programmes. The SIDO under Ministry of Industry sponsors training throughout the country with modified syllabi to suit the target groups. The central government has encouraged some of the state governments to conduct a number of programmes for members of scheduled caste/tribes. The National Backward Classes Development and Finance Corporation has of late, started similar activities for its beneficiaries. A large number of programmes are being conducted under the aegies of State Directorates of Industries throughout the country with District Industries Centre (DIC) as the pivot. The DICs conduct all training programmes related to Prime Ministers Rozgar Yojana (PMRY). The Technical Teaching Institutions under the patronage of Small Industries Development Bank of India (SIDBI) undertake such programmes for technology trained men and women on selective basis.

**Development of Entrepreneurship**

In short, entrepreneurship training aims to effect changes in the individual in terms of knowledge, attitude and skills, relevant to the entrepreneurship function. Persons may be trained for entrepreneurial careers so as to increase the level of confidence and achievement orientation. It is indeed, appreciable that the training programmes of the Government and Development

Banks have achieved a remarkable degree of success in creating a new class of industrial entrepreneurs. The National Institute of Small Industry Extension Training (NISIET) was set up at Hyderabad to provide extension training, mainly to the officers and field staff, working in various government departments, banks and non-government departments, banks and Non-governmental organisations so as to suit the specific requirements of the target groups. To encourage interaction between industry and institutes of science, technology, management and research, IDBI is extending assistance to projects for setting up "Science and Technology" Entrepreneurial Parks (STEPs). At present, there are nearly 690 organisations and institutions engaged in a variety of training and research programmes pertaining to development of entrepreneurship in the country.

**Entrepreneurship and Small Industry**

Small Industry sector plays a positive role in the development of entrepreneurs and managers. To promote and encourage entrepreneurship in small scale industry, the government has initiated many programmes and schemes. Small industry sector has enabled men with qualities of initiative, vision and leadership to become successful managers. It acts as a channel through which talented and motivated individuals can play a dynamic role. The success of small scale units largely depends on the technical knowledge of the entrepreneurs. It should be the endeavour of financial institutions and promotional bodies to attract entrepreneurs who have rich and varied exposure. The whole effort to promote and develop entrepreneurship primarily consists of three groups of activities, i.e., stimulatory, support and sustenance. All these are complementary to each other and they need assistance of many organisations and agencies.

**Entrepreneurship and Growth**

During the planning era covering a period of 45 years, Indian industrialisation has taken great strides in different fields along with a considerable development of human resources. It has been recognised that the entrepreneurial talents will accelerate the pace of India's development. The EDP has become an important policy instrument for human resource development. A country's development, economically and socially, could be achieved by the entrepreneurship traits. Diversification of Industries in various sectors of the economy is possible only by entrepreneurs. A developing country like India needs men of result orientation who can generate maximum production with minimum cost and with no wastage.

**Problems**

Despite that there has been a significant progress of entrepreneurship development in the last three decades, there are certain limiting factors which hinder the creation of nation-wide industrial entrepreneurial culture. The entrepreneurial field is still dominated by a few individuals and organisations. The government licences and other privileges have undoubtedly gone to selected established business houses. It can be said that entrepreneurial excellence in public sector enterprises has not gained the expected results. Another problem is that the number of sick units and the bank funds immobilised in small scale sector has grown rapidly. This is mainly due to the lack of suitable entrepreneurial talents alongwith other internal and external reasons. Further, there is a considerable difference between the type of entrepreneurship required for starting and running a business successfully and the methodology of entrepreneurship that is being imparted by the institutions.

**Strategies for Development of Entrepreneurship**

For a country like ours, which is striving to move from a predominantly agricultural society to an industrial society, entrepreneurship has an important role to play. Moreover, part of the solution to the growing unemployment, particularly among educated youth lies in such employment and entrepreneurship. There is a need to fix a target to train certain number of new entrepreneurs every year. In this regard the agencies required to impart complete training have to be identified. The State Directorates of Industries may be appointed to co-ordinate. The financial support required for the programmes will have to be provided by the central government through the national institutions set up for the purpose. A cross-section of the society can be categorised for selecting teams of trainees. Teams may be drawn from urban educated (men and women), Rural educated (men and women), Urban educated, rural uneducated, SC and ST (men and women), Artisans and professionals, women, etc. The course designed for the above groups is to be target specific. For uneducated entrepreneurs, the audio visual and demonstrative instructions would be found more effective.

It is high time that entrepreneurship be made a part of the university/college curriculam in addition to the entrepreneurship development programmes. There is a need to have a special programme below the graduate level (BBM) relating to entrepreneurship and management of small enterprises. The Government should encourage the formation of "Entrepreneurship Development Cell" in banks and other financial institutions to identify and help the entrepreneurs. The national institutions could supply the specific course material, training modules and other accessories.

Voluntary and Non-Governmental organisations should also work in close co-operation with financial institutions and government agencies in the process of creating a cadre of dedicated young men and women entrepreneurs. Public entrepreneurship has to be improved through better management and by giving due thrust on Research and Development in Public Sector undertakings. It is necessary that all training institutions/agencies and their training programmes be brought under the control of an apex body to be set up at the national level to co-ordinate and regulate the activities of all institutions engaged in the entrepreneurship programmes throughout the country. The apex body should have a mechanism for monitoring and evaluating the results of EDPs conducted for a diverse target group of entrepreneurs in the country. If EDPs are to succeed, it is necessary that emphasis is placed on adequate follow-up and supportive facilities for the entrepreneurs. A new generation of entrepreneurs will have to emerge to meet the increasing challenges of industry and trade.

# 19

# Entrepreneurial Traits and Skills: The Experience of Indian Entrepreneurs

—*Dr. R. Satya Raju*

## Introduction

Industrial Entrepreneurship is identified by many economists as a vital force in the process of industrialisation in general and economic development in particular. It is not enough to say that economic development is a function of land, labour, capital and technology. There must be some element to co-ordinate these factors in the right proportions, which is known as entrepreneurial ability. The entrepreneur is the central figure of any economic acitivity (George Herberta, 1949). The entrepreneurs are those, who initiate, organise, manage and control the affairs of business units that combine the factors of production to supply goods and services.

The economic development of a country is the function of effectiveness of entrepreneurship. If some countries like India have remained developing today, it is largely due to lack of adequate entrepreneurship. An entrepreneur is a person who buys factor services at certain prices with a view to sell its products at uncertain prices in the future (Kilby Peter, 1971).

## The Need

The existing literature on entrepreneurship has not focussed on the entrepreneurial skills or traits with reference to Indian environment. This paper seeks to examine the issues relating to entrepreneurial ventures in developing economies and the traits in India. It helps to bridge the research gap in the area of entrepreneurship.

### Objectives

The following are the main objectives:

*(a)* To review entrepreneurship programmes in developing economies.
*(b)* To examine entrepreneurial environment in India.
*(c)* To present entrepreneurial traits in Indian enterprises.

### Methodology

This paper is based on both primary and secondary sources of data. The data relating to entrepreneurship in developing economies and India was collected from the available literature in India. Primary data was collected by interviewing 150 entrepreneurs with a structured questionnaire. The responses were tabulated and briefly presented. This paper briefly reviews the issues relating to the International experiences, Indian experiences and the traits of successful Indian entrepreneurs.

### Major Observations

Research studies reveal that the persons possessing industrial or commercial experience have been far more successful in their business. Self-employment provides useful ground for success in organised manufacturing enterprises. Similarly, employment experience on technical or non technical areas provides necessary motivation, and essential business exposure or industrial orientation.

In Malaysia, the entrepreneurship programmes have been attracting school dropouts, small traders, employees, artisans, craftsmen and women. MARA is striving hard for rural self-employment programmes in Malaysia. In Sri Lanka, the Chamber of Small Industry conducts entrepreneurship programmes regularly. The Ministry of Youth Affairs in Sri Lanka conducts short term programmes for creating awareness about self-employment among school and college dropouts and gives preliminary information on accounts, management, marketing, etc. An autonomous institute was set up within the University of Philippines for Small Scale Industries, which is recognised as a focal point of expertise and resource for entrepreneurship programmes. The new entrepreneurs in Philippines have successfully developed handicrafts sector. The Asian Institute of Management (AIM) has a clear objective that the students must become entrepreneurial managers rather than management executives. Students are encouraged to take up projects which they conceptualise, set up and successfully run and then report their experiences, instead of writing a thesis. A good number of students chose to set up successful enterprises because of this option. Thus, AIM helps to develop a culture for enterprise building in the Business School.

In Australia, schools offer programmes for managing the enterprises; whereas in Jamaica, Zambia, Switzerland, Uganda, Sierra Leone, New Guinea and Zimbabwe the entrepreneurship programmes are encouraged by the respective governments. The international research project had identified Personal Entrepreneurial Characteristics (PECs) by studying the tasks, activities and behaviour of successful and average entrepreneurs of India. The important entrepreneurial career among all the three countries would include achievement cluster; thinking and problem solving cluster; personal maturity cluster; influence cluster and directing and controlling cluster. Some characteristics were—persistence; information seeking; concern for high quality work; commitment to work; efficiency; initiation; systematic planning; problem solving; self-confidence; etc. The entrepreneurial traits which were assessed in the behaviour tests were: the need to achieve and desire to achieve some standards of excellence; self confidences; initiative and independence; problem solving tendency; in search of positive environment; goal setting under strategic planning and implementation.

Until the mid 20th century, the development of entrepreneurship was very slow in India because the regulation of British Rule did not encourage industrial ventures. The need for entrepreneurship development was first felt only after introducing the Industrial Policy Resolutions in 1948 and 1956. The Industrial Policy Resolution of 1956 specified the fields of activity for private sector enterprises.

In India, Entrepreneurship Development Programmes are

sponsored by the State Governemnts, Industrial promotion organisations and development banks to achieve one or more of the following objectives:

(*a*) Accelerated industrial development by enlarging the supply of entrepreneurs.
(*b*) Industrial development of rural and less developed areas, where local entrepreneurship is not readily available and entrepreneurs from nearby cities and towns are not easily attracted.
(*c*) Enlarging the small and medium enterprises sector which offers better potential for employment generation and wider dispersal of industrial ownership.
(*d*) Providing productive self-employment to a number of educated and less educated young men and women coming out of schools and colleges.
(*e*) Improving performance of small industries by enlarging the supply of carefully selected and trained well rounded entrepreneurs and diversifying sources of entrepreneurship.

The performance of the State Entrepreneurship Development Institute (EDI)s in India is as following: Centre for Entrepreneurship Development, Karnataka (CEDOK), Bangalore has conducted 196 programmes during 1992-93 and 1994-95 for 7,423 beneficiaries. The Centre for Entrepreneurship Development (CED), Lucknow, has conducted 336 programmes for 11,226 beneficiaries during 1992-94. The Centre for Entrepreneurship Development (CED), Madurai has provided training for 104 programmes during 1992-95. The Institute for Entrepreneurship Development (IED), Bhubaneshwar has conducted training to 984 persons during 1992-93. The Centre for Entrepreneurship Development (CED), Bhopal has conducted 231 programmes for 6,053 beneficiaries during 1993-94.

Small Industries Management Development Programmes (MDPs) are conducted by small Industries Service Institutes throughout the country. MDPs are designed to benefit the small industry entrepreneurs and supervisory personnel in sharpening their management skills.

National Institute of Small Industry Extension Training (NISIET) is an autonomous body functioning under the purview of Ministry of Industry. NISIET organises training for small industry entrepreneurs, officers, State/Central Government and international programmes. NISIET also takes up small industries research and consultancy work for central and state Government organisations and others.

Integrated Training Centre (ITC) has been functioning from 1963 under the purview of Small Industries Development Organisation. ITC imparts training to Industrial Extension Officers of State Governments and organises Rural Entrpreneurship cum skill Development programmes for the youth from rural areas. ITC conducts training courses for the officers of District Industries Centres and Block Development Officers and orientation training courses for junior officers of Small Industries, Ahmedabad. ITC which is promoted by the Indian financial institutions, has also been conducting several programmes to encourage entrepreneurs and also to provide skills and expertise to manage their enterprises.

As per the existing literature, entrepreneurs are from different linguistic communities in India. Most of them are Gujaratis; Marathis; Punjabis; Marwaris; Tamilians; Andhras and Malayalis. Many are Hindus, followed by Muslims and Christians. Among them Sardarjis, Brahmins, Kshatriyas, Patels, Jains, Vaidyas are prominent. In Andhra Pradesh, the main entrepreneurial communities are Vaidyas, Kammas, Reddys, Brahmins, and Kapus.

As per the study conducted by the researchers, successful entrepreneurs are above 40 years of age. They acquired skills and managerial abilities from their parents or friends. Most of the entrepreneurs are from lower middle and middle class. Their educational background was low. The entrepreneurs had a desire to train their children in the same line of activity and their intention was to entrust the business as their successors. The enterprises in India were proprietory, partnership, private and public sector companies. The entrepreneurs being limited had the problems of raw materials shortage; non- availability of raw materials; improper working capital management; lack of marketing and infrastructural facilities which were the main reasons for industrial sickness among several enterprises.

The entrepreneurial traits of the successful entrepreneurs in India are as following: Professionalism, innovative thinking, high knowledge, quality consciousness (Lakhsmanbhai R. Gandhi and

Ramachandrabhai R. Gandhi of Vadilal Ice Cream); affordable price, smart pricing strategy, developing mass market (Karsanbhai K Patel of Nirma Chemical Works); fair price, strong marketing strategies (Aspi R. Balsara of Balsara Hygiene Products); pursuit of excellence, grow or perish policy, internationalism (K.M. Mammen Mappilai of M.R.F.); to be number one in all respects (A.K. Mukherjee and Asho Aikat of Sonodyne Electronics); honesty, dedication, Japanese culture, innovations (Jyothi Mukherjee of Bharat Biscuits); commitment, technology and vision (Chandramohan of Punjab Tractors), satisfying customer, employing women (Satya Prakash Mathur of Sumeet); service to society through industry, sacrificing nature (K.V.K. Raju of Nagarjuna Steels); innovation, loyalty to customers, commitment to quality (Ramanbai B. Patel and Indravadan A. Modi of Cadila Laboratories); employee co-operation, customer support (P. Rangachar of Yeken India).

A recent study in India revealed that due consideration is given to the attributes of leadership abilities, profit orientation, ability to attract and retain talent, best industrial relations policies, honesty, ability to establish an international presence for choosing the best chief executives. The study further stated that the best chief executives were : Ratan Tata (Tata Sons); K.L. Chugh (I.T.C.); Ambani (Reliance Industries); S.M. Daita (Hind Lever): Birla A. (Indian Rayon), Bajaj R. (Bajaj Auto); Seth D. (Tata Chemicals); Godrej A.B. (Godrej), Irani J.J. (Tata Steel); Thapar L.M. (Crompton Greaves); Goenka H.V. (R.P.G. Enter-prises); Nusli Wadia (Bombay Dyeing); Vijay Mallya (U.B. Group); Chhabaria M.R. (Shaw Wallace).

## Conclusion

Several attempts were made to promote enterpreneurship in India. The entrepreneurs possess different traits. All the traits are acquired through their experience, interaction with people and also inheritance. Though the government of India has introduced several measures, still it has to play a greater role in encouraging entrepreneurship in different activities by imparting education at various levels of study on the skills and traits required for successful management. The support should be continuous at all levels. The need of the hour is to establish a separate Ministry for Entrepreneurship Development at the central and state levels.

As most of the enterprises are growing concerns, appropriate strategies are to be adopted for diversifying the business activities. Depending upon the environmental analysis, they have to adopt appropriate strategies. The entrepreneurial development is required in India by following the Panchsheel of development which includes awakening; education; organisation; empowerment; action and programme. The entrepreneurs should understand that they cannot do today's job with yesterday's method and be in tomorrows business.

## References

Fredrick, B., *History and Structure of Economic Development*, Oxford and IBH Publishing Company, New Delhi, 1969.

George Herberta Evans Jr., "The Entrepreneur and Economic Theory", *American Economic Review*, 1949.

Government of India, Planning Commission, *Seventh Five Year Plan*, the author, New Delhi, 1985.

Government of India, Ministry of Industry, *Planning for Development of Small Scale Industries*, New Delhi.

Kilby Peter, (Ed.), *Entrepreneurship and Economic Development*, Free Press, New York, 1971.

Satya Raju, R., *Urban Unorganised Sector in India*, Mittal Publishers, New Delhi, 1989.

"Training for Women Entrepreneurship" Paper presented at the National Seminar on *Women and Rural Entrepreneurship – A Strategic Planning Approach*, at Madurai Kamraj University, Madurai, during 5–6 September, 1990.

*Entrepreneurship in Small Enterprises*, Deptt. of Commerce and Management Studies, Andhra University, Vishakhapatnam, 1994 (Mimeo).

Tandon, B.C., *Environment and Entrepreneur*, Chaugh Prakashan, Allahabad, 1975.

William J. Bowmal, "Entrepreneurship in Economic Theory", *American Economic Review*, May, 1968, 58 (2).

# 20

# Small Entrepreneurial Education—Approach and Methodology

*—Dr. Khursheed A. Bhat*

Nations become economically great not because of natural resources but because of quality of entrepreneurial talent with which endowed. The rich natural resource base only provides a comparative advantage for industries based on these resources but, it is the reservoir of rich entrepreneurial talent which exploits the resources and invents new methods and consumptions, thus guarantees the success in Industrialisation. Entrepreneur who is a front line actor in the process of Industrial development, with his dynamism, ability and ingenuity, brings a change in the socio-economic order (Bhat, 1998). Economic Development originates and fosters in relation to the strengths and health of the entrepreneurship and depends upon the rate of its generation and equally to the intensity of its scene of social responsibility, its inventive quotient and its index of management capabilities (McClelland, 1985). Sufficient research evidences have also revealed that there exists significant relationship between entrepreneurial talent and economic growth (Mathur, 1989). Most glaring example in this regard is of the industrially developed states of the world like, US and Japan, which have achieved phenomenal economic growth largely due to quality entrepreneurship though not rich in natural resources in particular, Japan. However, entrepreneurial talent is not the domain of any country or race, but can be developed anywhere which calls for well designed, planned interventions and presence of efficient and sufficient support system. Once the entrepreneurial culture is fully developed, then it strengthens its bonds itself.

**Born or Made: 20 : 40 : 40 Dimension**

Are entrepreneurs born or made? Earlier economists and sociologists viewed that entrepreneurs are born and not made. Today strong belief that lies in the Myth that the entrepreneurs are born and not made no longer exists. "Experiences of past few decades both in India and abroad clearly shows that it is possible to develop entrepreneurs through planned efforts" (Shugumar, 1966). The same view has been expressed by Khullar, *et al.*, 1966; Mathur, 1979) Singh, 1989 and Bhat, 1997. The fact of the matter is that the entrepreneurs are born as well can be made. Entrepreneurship is a talent, native genius and born insight, however, unless this native genius and born insight is awakened and sharpened, encouraged and supported, the born talent is unlikely to act as a "spark plug" to transform economic scene and bring a new dynamism in it (Bhat, 1997). Generally every region/society is based on 20:40:40 dimension with plus-minus variations from region to region, specifying that 20 per cent of the people are born with desire and talent for entrepreneurship and need not to be awakened, but needs proper support system; 40 per cent of the people have the capacity and capability to become successful entrepreneurs but this group needs to be enthused and developed. Another group of 40 per cent either got no capacity or interest for entrepreneurship. So it would be feasible to identify first the middle group and develop and sharpen their skills. Further, experiments conducted all over India, as also in the Asia Pacific region brought out that the "right personality, calibre, motivation, willingness to learn and venturesomeness are more important for entrepreneurial success than mere formal education attainments" (Singh, 1989). However, better educatio-nal attainments provide better chances to learn, exploit and grow. To create and develop entrepreneurial talent in the country, the need is to motivate and identify the talent; educate, train and sponsor them.

**Promotional Handicaps**

While there has been sufficient growth in small entrepreneurship in the country in the last 25-30 years, yet it is still comparatively scarce factor as indeed in all developing economies (Desai, 1995). The country is fortunate to be well endowed with plentiful natural and human resources, however, it could not witness the emergence of sufficient, quality and sustainable entrepreneurship, because of which the country is still reeling under economic under-development. The number of small scale units in the country stood at 2.5 million as on 1995 as compared to 14 million in US and 5 million in Japan. In spite of being very large in size and rich in natural and human resources in comparision to these industrially developed countries of the world, the country could not witness the emergence of sufficient and quality entrepreneurship. More intriming aspect of small entrepreneurship in the country has been the presence of widespread sickness and large number of "Ghost units" in the small scale sector which has also been reported due to the absence of genuine and self motivated entrepreneurs. The number of sick units as on March, 1995 stood at 3.94 lakh, having Rs. 15733 crores outstanding with banks. Of these 3.91 lakh units including weak units belong to small scale sector which account for nearly 99 per cent of the total sick industrial units in the country. Besides, there are 1.49 lakh SSI units with an outstanding bank credit of Rs. 1881 crores, which are not traceable. The number of untraceable units in the sector are on rise. Various obstacles have been identified inhibiting the development of sustainable small entrepreneurship in the country. Absense of objective oriented entrepreneur manager; lack of technical guidance and support; incomplete and inefficient support system; unrealistic policies and programmes and above all the absence of a political resolve and confusion have roadblocked the development of small scale sector in the country to its fullest potential and on sound lines (Bhat, 1997 and Joshi, 1991).

Entrepreneurial motives, abilities and a congenial environment which promotes the development of sustainable small entrepreneurship, have been found to be largely lacking in the country (Desai, 1995). The enterprising youth in the country largely are lacking preference for entrepreneurship and are heavily oriented towards Government jobs, which in turn has caused serious unemployment problem (Bhat, 1997). It is also true that a large number of people have assumed small entrepreneurship just to obtain institutional finances and pocket away incentives and subsidies. Many more have assumed entrepreneurship either due to wave of industry or were unable to get government job. Further, the small entrepreneurship obtaining in the country apart from being limited, most of it does not appear to appreciate the significance and utility of the modern business practices. This has been found largely due to the lack of right amount of knowledge, understanding, vision, exposure, industrial conception and proper support system. Most of the entrepreneurs have been found not possessing even a rudimentary knowledge of managerial aspects and because of which their approach has remained conservative rather than scientific and forward and outward looking.

The abovesaid state of affairs has been found largely due to the unplanned, incomplete and unrealisitic promotional methodologies adopted in the development of sustainable entrepreneurship in the country. Ill planned training methodology, inconsistency in programme design, its content, sequence and theme and the focus of the programme is not clear, thus failed to yield desired results (Khuller, 1996). The poor implementation of the industrial policies and programmes has added to the problem. The system of education that the country followed right from independence has failed to foster the desire of entrepreneurship among the educated youth. Given the above facts, if the country has to witness the emergence of quality small entrepreneurship in a big way, it needs to create a highly motivated and result oriented "entrepreneur-Manager cadre" with outward and forward looking approach which calls for systematic and well thought planned intervention in the direction of entrepreneurial education, training and creating efficient and sufficient support system. Since the motives and entrepreneurial zeal is largely absent among the educated youth, hence the creation of congenial environment should be at the top of everything, thus causing a catalytic role for the government and its sponsored agencies. Each group of activities is highly interactive, supplementary and crucial to the others. Underemphasis of one or the other activity will render the whole process infructuous and the end result will be birth of a large number of small enterprises with equally growing percentage of sickness as has been happening till date.

### *1. Creating Achievement Motivation*

The characteristics of entrepreneurship are gamblers instinct and may be, a certain degree of ruthlessness for achieving results as per the plans plus industrial conception knowledge, vision, dynamism and meticulous planning (Desai, 1995). David C. McClelland of Harward University has established a correlation between economic growth and the entrepreneurial ability displayed by the society in terms of motivation, etc. Experiments conducted in India in this regard also reveal close correspondence in the relationship between motivation and entrepreneurial success, conditioned by the sufficient and efficient support system (Mehta, 1996). Motivation is nothing but a desire to achieve a goal. It is this strong urge for achievement that acts as a true motivator. But this motivation is basic to entrepreneurial ability. So before identifying the potential entrepreneurs, there is a great need to create a strong desire for achievement in entrepreneurship in the people in general. The strong desire for entrepreneurship can be created by evolving vigorous publicity; reorientation of social behaviours, creating success stories to act as a role model and above all attuning the education system to foster entrepreneurship.

#### *1a. Vocationalisation of Entrepreneurial Education*

Colleges and the universities are the right places to get the budding and potential entrepreneurs. However, the present system of education in the country is not attuned to foster entrepreneurship rather, it is producing an army of white collared job seekers. The existing curriculum in polytechnics and other institutions does not prepare students to opt for entrepreneurship (Saini *et al.*, 1996). To foster a taste for entrepreneurship at an early stage, there is an immediate need to restructure the curriculum in a way so as to entrepreneurise the education system both technical and non-technical. Whatever, efforts has been made towards encouraging entrepreneurship through formal education in some states, is ad hoc in nature and half hearted effort, thus has failed to result in entrepreneurship. Special emphasis should be laid on the development of entrepreneurial skills, so that instead of looking only for government jobs which are scarce, the students can look for small entrepreneurship, hence entrepreneurship development should one of the primary goals of education (Fayyaz, 1998). The introduction of entrepreneurship development as one of the subjects in three year degree course would provide a sufficient basis for the development of entrepreneurial zeal among the educated youth. More appropriate would be to introduce vocational course on small entrepreneurship in all the colleges and the interested students from all streams be allowed to take up the course. Initially counselling to the students should attain the equal importance.

*1b. Entrepreneurial Awareness Programmes*

Formal educational attainments have little to do with the successful entrepreneurship. Entrepreneurs can be found in any strata of the society. In Japan entrepreneurs (innovators) are from the under-privileged classes largely, it is because of the fact that this class got a strong urge to achieve the economic affluence (Desai, 1995). People in general in the country lack information about the entrepreneurial opportunities, schemes, incentives, etc., which has been found to be acting as one of the deterring factors for choosing the industrial entrepreneurship at the time of choosing their careers (Mehta 1996). Present state of affairs is that most of the entrepreneurs have choosen it a career of last resort. Wrong selection of target groups has contributed largely to the failure of a number of EDP's. Well designed and properly executed publicity campaign for entrepreneurship opportunities would enable to enthuse and surface the entrepreneurial zeal/talent. The entrepreneurial awareness interactive programmes should be conducted by the different promotional agencies on continuous basis. Mass media in todays contemporary world can also play its role in these awareness programmes. Better means to conduct awareness programmes would be to create "Entrepreneurial Development Cell" in various colleges and universities to act as a data bank and a counsellor to the students. However, such cells should be created and supported by the various promotional agencies together so as to make them meaningful rather than an academic formality. Instead of waiting for the prospective entrepreneurs to approach, the practice of selecting the potential entrepreneurs at their doorsteps should be followed. They can then be educated, trained, guided, helped and supported during the pre-and post-stages of actual entrepreneurship.

*1c. Strategies for Creating Achievement Motivation*

Mere vocationalisation of entrepreneurship education and awareness programmes would do nothing concrete unless, proper strategies are formulated to entrepreneurise the minds of the educated youth in particular. The following few strategies are recommended in this context.

- Provide various concessions and incentives to the entrepreneurs and some specifically to the highly educated entrepreneurs.
- Create sufficient and efficient support system.
- Ensure right type of opportunity guidance, etc., which calls for identifying the potential lines of activity with all other details.
- Ensure sufficient credit of varied nature at lower rate of interest.
- Develop industrially important infrastructural facilities .
- Help in conducting techno-economic feasibility studies.
- Sponsor and guide in the initial stages of development.
- Minimise paper work and procedure so as to streamline the follow up of incentives, etc.
- Save the entrepreneurs from the hassles of multi-office environment.

**2. *Education and Skill Development***

McClelland had observed that with proper training provided to the right kind of persons, sustainable entrepreneurship could be developed. In this regard, an experiment was conducted in the towns of Andhra Pradesh in collaboration with Small Industry Extension Training Institute, where some young businessmen were given a two week orientation course, designed to stimulate the imagination, etc. The result of the study has revealed that the trainees displayed a more active behaviour, worked long hours, started new ventures, etc. (Mathur, 1979). In a workshop organised by the East-West Centre Technology Institute, Hawaii, the EDP experiences of various countries were discussed which revealed that training made a lot of difference in the performance of entrepreneurs. Although, it is a universal fact, that the training and education of potential entrepreneurs has a significant bearing on the successful pursuits of entrepreneurship, yet the question that arises is what training inputs are needed by the potential entrepreneurs. Small industry thinkers and researchers have identified the different training inputs required to be imparted to the potential entrepreneurs to make them competent and capable. Behavioural competence like, intra-punitive competencies, initiative and risk taking capacities are required for successfully managing an industrial enterprise (Sugmar, 1996). However, Akhouri and Mishra (1996), observed that entrepreneurial values, attitudes and motivations give rise to several personal competencies which are practised throughout the entrepreneurial career, starting from identification and selection to launching, management and growth of an enterprise. The small entrepreneur over and above creating, initiating and risk taking, acts as a "think tank", the "production supervisor," the "marketeer" the "plant secretary" and thus needs to discharge diverse functions in todays highly dynamic and competitive business world (Bhat, 1997). Given the domain of small entrepreneurs and the emerging industrial scene, the small entrepreneurs have to grow as "multipreneurs" shedding some of their inherent weaknesses and inhibitions and expand their domain of success (Raju, 1996). From the above discussions it can be concluded that the small entrepreneurs have to discharge twin functions of an "entrepreneur" and "multifarious manager". So the need is to make them:

- Highly knowledgeable with great vision and dynamism. Know the different incentives, concessions and other facilities being offered to small scale industries and the procedures thereof.
- Understand the different laws, regulations and procedures to be followed in the establishment of an enterprise, etc.
- Develop entrepreneurial values, attitudes and motivations and making them to understand the behavioural competencies required for successful entrepreneurship.
- Understand the importance of financial discipline at all times.
- Knowledge of the different stages of growth of an enterprise and how to meet competition.
- Develop workable technical and managerial skills. More

emphasis should be on the transformation of potential entrepreneurs into a disciplined and management knowing persons with outward and forward looking approach. Creating and sharpening of marketing skills should attain the top prioirty.

- How to get finances and planning of capital expenditures.
- How to forge good relations with different individuals and organisations looking after industrial development.
- How to seize an opportunity and thereof conduct market-surveys/studies and details regarding preparation of project-cum-feasibility report.

The whole programme of entrepreneurial education, training and development can be broadly grouped into six modules, viz., achievement motivation, education, development of managerial training skills, project planning and implementation, organisation of business and management of growth and competition. The programme is a continuous process and a step by step process, one preceding the other. There should not be overlaping of process. The programme should include lectures, discussions, workshop exercises, case studies and real life experiences. Prominent industrialists should also be involved in the programme.

*2a. Entreprenuurial Circles*

Unless the marriage between theory and practice is attained the training programmes are unlikely to deliver the best results. To make the programmes meaningful and result oriented, the potential entrepreneurs after achievement motivation, managerial and technical training, etc., should be exposed to real life experiences during the training programmes on the pattern of British Training Model. The potential entrepreneurs during the programme should be allowed to form "Entrepreneurial Circles" and authorise them to choose the product, arrange raw materials, manufacture, market their products and prepare and submit reports. In this regard, they need financial and manufacturing facility support, thus requiring the institute/agency conducting such programmes, to create a fund and manufacturing facilities for the same. The success in these innovative programmes would depend largely on the efficiency of the agency organising such programmes.

*2b. Entrepreneurial Development Institutes*

Entrepreneurial Development Institute would be an ideal agency to conduct training programmes. The Institute should consist of three divisions, viz., Research and Development, Training and Statistics and Evaluation. However, the analysis of the performance of the existing institutes in the country has not remained rosy and worth mentioning. Although, no worthwhile study has been conducted on the efficiency of the working of these institutes; yet, it is generally agreed that these have also failed due to poor linkages. Given this fact, the institutes on the lines of developed countries like US, etc., should work in union with other agencies operating in the environment of small scale industries and enter into partnership with the universities, engineering colleges, polytechnics and research institutions in the process of developing small entrepreneurship. Apart from the traditional role, the universities, etc., can be made to play an important role in promoting entrepreneurship in their areas of operations where they enjoy technical and other informations and expertise. In the US, State Universities have contributed much to the promotion of industrial activity by helping in innovations and by organising "incubators".

*2c. Parent-Child Approach*

"Small is beautiful" but at the same time, is weak thus vulnerable to many risks and threats when left unattended. Same is true with small entrepreneurs. As soon as the small entrepreneurs come into existence they cannot be left to the onslaughts of the hostile business world which is highly complex for which they are weak and inexperienced to stand with. However, under the present system, the small entrepreneur gets birth without parents. As a result, most of the small scale units die as a "still born child" in the absence of proper nursing and planning (Reddy, 1993). Born sickness and the sickness due to faulty project planning and implementation is very much prevelent in the small scale sector in the country, which has been reported due to the absence of proper guidance and support to budding entrepreneurs during pre- and post-stages of development (Bhat, 1997, Mohrana *et al.*, 1991, Panda *et al.*, 1992). It is also due to the fact that the industrial scene in India is dominated by family industrial houses like, Tata's, Birla's Godrej, etc. Research evidences have also revealed that family background has a greater influence on the suggested pursuits in entrepreneurship as the budding and potential entrepreneurs develop greater urge, get proper counselling, guidance and support in the initial stages of development from their parents who are with rich business experiences. This glaring evidence further cements the need for creating parents (counsellors, guide, etc.), in the environment of small scale entrepreneurs who are otherwise weak and inexperienced.

The law of nature also states that small needs a parent who will guide, counsel, support and help till he grows late maturity. In US "Incubators" are used successfully to develop small entrepreneurship wherein, advisory services, and support is offered and provided on the subjects with which most budding entrepreneurs are unfamiliar (Desai, 1995). Given the inherent weakness of the small entrepreneurs, the Entrepreneurial Development Institutes should also act as "consultants" (Parent) thus guide, counsel, and help the small entrepreneurs (child) in:

- Project planning and implementation,
- Capacity planning,
- Selecting and acquiring technology,
- Organising the enterprise and in acquiring various licences and certificates,
- Product design, engineering and development,
- Acquiring finances and designing capital structure,
- Pilot production and quality management,
- Vendor development and product launching,
- Framing market programmes and strategies and organising sales network,
- Managing growth and competition.

The following few suggestions are also expected to go a long way to help the emergence of quality small entrepreneurship:

- Private sector companies should also be involved in the process of small entrepreneurship development. The private companies be motivated to develop "incubators" with the purpose to guide, counsel, help and support the small entrepreneurship in their own areas of specialisation. This would also help them to develop suppliers of small parts of their requirements.

- Encourage creation of professional and competent key individual consultants/firms.
- Professionalise the management of DICs. More better would be to handover DIC's to industrial consultants with adequate authority and facilities.
- The practice of short tenure bureaurcratic heads should be replaced by the permanent heads, having specialization in the fields of finance. However, such appointments should be allowed to manage without any political interference and given greater degree of autonomy in decision making.

*3. Sponsors*

The Entrepreneurial Development Institute should also act as a "consultant" to the small scale industries. As such it should in no case feel that it is absolved of its duties and responsibilities once the training programme is over. Now the time has come to think seriously that their role should not be restricted to knowledge input, opportunity guidance, etc. They should be made to provide a back up support to the extent possible (Bhat, 1998). In order to ensure an equal treatment to the small scale industries by the banks, SFC's and service organisations, the institute should sponsor them. To allow the institute to play its role of a sponsorer effectively, there is a need for some empowerment. Empowerment may be in the manner that they "sponsor" or act on behalf of the prospective entrepreneurs. Every entrepreneur who gets training in the institute should be treated as a member of the institute for the purpose of sponsorship.

**Catalyst**

Industrialisation in effect is a role play of different role players (organisations and individuals), but the role play by the government in generating necessary impulse towards entrepreneurship is widespread and catalytic. It is the responsibility of the government and the sponsoring agencies to create congenial environment and efficient and sufficient support system which would itself encourage potential entrepreneurs and others to play their roles more seriously and effectively. "In US, State authorities enabled businessmen to cut through red-tap, provide low interest loans to develop prototypes, undertake market research and generally assist in bringing a new product. Some notion of the magnitude of this support can be had from the fact that in the year 1997-98 alone the federal and state governments together spent more than $2000 million in encouraging small businesses (Desai, 1995). To promote sustainable small entrepreneurship in the country, the government's have assumed a multifaceted role of financier, marketeer, supplier, trainer, guide, counsellor and regulator. The roles of government can broadly be classified into the promotional and regulatory. The regulatory role has to be minimum and subservient to the promotional role. The regulations are meant for avoiding the misuse of incentives and concessions and at the same time for ensuring that different incentives are delivered to the genuine entrepreneurs in time and with ease.

A close introspection of the role performance of different organisations operating in the environment of SSI in the country brings to light the inadequacy of role performance. How rich or financially sound the different organisations looking after the small industrial development in the country may be, they still suffer from various forms of corporate ill health. The financial and service organisations and administered more than strategically managed. Their culture is that of bureaucratic maze than that of a risk taking entrepreneur (Hedge *et al.*, 1988). More intriguing aspect about these organisations has been that these have misconstrued their role of a promoter and are obsessed with the regulatory role, thus and rules in favour of flexible organisational structures. Managers in these organisations lack autonomy and entrepreneurship, right attitudes, commitment and industrial conception which is also coming in the way of managing industrial programmes strategically and with vigour (Bhat, 1997). Further, the different incentives and concessions are not being delivered to the genuine entrepreneurs in time and easily. At the same time, the subsidy culture has breeded insincere and bogus entrepreneurs and many evils in the administrative set up (Deolanker, 1985). So in the process of strengthening the support system for small entrepreneurship development, there is an equal need to set the existing organizations in right shape: rewrite their promotional methodologies; merge and create some new roles in the context of new economic milieu and restructure and re-organise the package of incentives so as to streamline their flow to the genuine entrepreneurs with minimum of paper work. All this would require to rationalise the mind set of industrial planners and administrators who suffer from many misconceptions about entrepreneurship development.

## Conclusion

Small entrepreneurship dovetail well with the economic imperatives of the country. Although, there has been sufficient growth in small entrepreneurship yet, it is still a scarce factor and mared by many inhibitions. Absence of entrepreneurial motives, abilities and congenial environment to promote sustainable small entrepreneurship has greatly impeded the development of small entrepreneurship in the country. This has largely been due to the fact that the methodologies in vogue for entrepreneurial education and skill development are not well planned and lack focus. Absence of focus to foster entrepreneurship in formal education has also contributed its bit.

To develop competent and capable small entrepreneurs, is a three-tier process, viz., creating achievement motivation, education and skill development and guide and support during pre and post training stages. Vocationalisation of entrepreneurial education and well designed entrepreneurship awareness programmes would help to create achievement motivation in entrepreneurship among the people in particular, educated youth. Universities, EDIs, engineering colleges and other institutions in collaboration with various financial and service organisations have a greater role to play in fostering and development entrepreneurship. To sustain and accelerate its rate of generation, there is a need to create consultants, sponsors and sufficient and efficient support system. The government has to act as a catalyst in creating congenial environment for entrepreneurial growth and development. Given the existing institutional framework and its state of role performance, there is a great need to take some bold initiatives in rewriting their promotional methodologies, removing the malpractices and in merging and creating some new role players.

## References

1. Bhat, K.A. (1997), "*Industrial Sickness in modern small scale Industries in J & K State.*" Ph.D. Thesis submitted to Kashmir University.
2. McClelland, D.C. (1985), *Motivating Economic Achievement*, New York, The Free Press.
3. Mathur, S.P. (1979), *Economics of Small Scale Industries*, Sundeep Prakashan, Delhi.
4. Sugmar, M. (1996), "Entrepreneurial Competence among Small Entrepreneurs", *Small Enterprises Development, Management and Extension Journal (SEDME)*, NISIET, Hyderabad Vol. XXIII, No. 4.
5. Khullar, J.S. and Ranjit Singh (1996), "Strategies for Entrepreneurship Development", *Small Enterprises Development Management and Extention Journal (SEDME)*, NISIET, Hyderabad, Vol. XXIII, No. 2.
6. Singh, N.P. (1989), "Entrepreneurship Development: Some Thoughts", *MDI Management Journal*,Vol. 2, No. 1.
7. Desai, V. (1995), *Dynamics of Entrepreneurial Development and Management*, Himalaya Publishing House, Mumbai.
8. Joshi, V.K. (1991), "Analysis of Causes of Industrial Sickness Management of Industrial Sickness", *The Management Accountant*.
9. Arunachalam, S. (1993), "Sickness in Small Industries Growth and Analysis", *Industrial Sickness*, edited by Ramakant *et al.*, Pointer Publishers, Jaipur.
10. Reddy, K.C. (1993), *Sickness in Small Scale Industries*, Ashish Publishing House, New Delhi.
11. Mehta, P. (1996), "Fostering Creative Response, Innovativeness and Entrepreneurship : Some Thoughts for Discussion", *Small Enterprise Development Management and Extention Journal (SEDME)*, NISIET, Hyderabad, Vol. XXIII, No. 2.
12. Saini, J.S. and Sharma D.D. (1996), "Entrepreneur Technical Education Curriculum", *Small Enterprises Development, Management and Extensions Journal (SEDME)*, NISIET, Hyderabad, Vol. XXIII, No. 2.
13. Akhouri, M.M.P. and Mishra, S.P. (1996), "Entrepreneurship Education: A Conceptual Base, Approach and Methodology", *Indian Management*, No. V, pp. 53-65.
14. Raju, E.B., (1996), "From Entrepreneurship to Multipreneurship", *Small Enterprises Development, Management and Extension Journal (SEDME)*, NISIET, Hyderabad, Vol. XXIII, No. 4.
15. Mohrana, S. and Gana R. (1991), "Sickness in Small Scale Sector—The Role of Commerical Banks", *Industrial Sickness*, edited by P. Nagaiya, Discovery Publishing House, New Delhi.
16. Panda, R.K. and Kishore, M. (1992), *Industrial Sickness : Study of Small Scale Industries*, Ashish Publishing House, New Delhi.
17. Bhat, K.A. (1998), "Small Entrepreneurial Development : Model for 21st Century : A Case Study of J & K State".

18. Hedge, M.G., Mishra, R.K. and Bhat, K.S. (1989), "Actors and Factors in Industrial Sickness in India", *Sickness in Small Scale Industries*, edite by Reddy *et al.*, Himalaya Publishing House, Mumbai.
19. Deolankar, V.S. (1985), "Industrial Sickness in Small Scale Industries in India", *Indian Journal of Commerce*, Vol. XXXVIII, Part 1, No. 142.
20. Fayyaz, S.A. (1998), "Vocationalisation of Business Education in Kashmir: Implementation, Constraints and Opportunities", *The Business Review*, Vol. 4, Nos. 1 and 2.

# 21

# Entrepreneurship in Tribal Areas

—*Dr. I. Parthasarathi*

The present paper seeks to examine the economic status of Tribal and Non-Tribal entrepreneurs, reasons for their entry into business and the problems faced by them in procurement of funds and sale of goods. Provision of institutions credit at lower rates of interest, strict vigil of higher officials on the field staff and Girijan Corporation, provision of shopping complexes at places where people congregate instead of at far off places are suggested to help the entrepreneurs, improve their economic status and well being.

In economic theory and history, it has been recognised that accumulation of physical resources is a major element in the process of economic development. Further recent studies of industrialised nations have brought out the equally crucial role played by accumulation of human capital. In recent years, human resources development has been receiving great attention in developing countries and with this came renewed attention towards the role of entrepreneurship in initating and stimulating economic development. It is now well recognised that an adequate supply of able and well motivated entrepreneurs is a pre-condition for accelerating the process of economic development.

Though the role of entrepreneurs in initiating and stimulating the process of economic development is well recognised, studies on entrepreneurship are somewhat rare. Further empirical studies on entrepreneurship in tribal areas are almost conspicuous by its absence, as tribal areas are generally backward due to factors like topography and terrain as well as illiteracy and innocence of the people. Against this background, an attempt is being made in this paper to study some of the aspects of entrepreneurship in tribal areas purposively selecting the tribal strip of Paderu Mandal of Andhra Pradesh. The main objective of the present paper is to study the economic status of the tribal and non-tribal entrepreneurs and highlight the problems being faced by them in the running of their enterprises.

**Database and Methodology**

The present study is based on data gathered from primary sources. The primary data are gathered from the offices of the Mandal Revenue Officer, Paderu Mandal, Project Officer. Integrated Tribal Development Agency, Paderu; District Educational Officer (Agency), Paderu; and also from a well structured schedule administered to entrepreneurs. For the purpose of administering the schedules, the following procedure is adopted.

The population of Paderu Mandal is 44,875 as per 1991 census comprising of Tribals and Non-Tribals in the ratio of 4:1. The records of the Mandal Revenue Officer reveal that there are 2,989 persons in other occupations and 1998 are in business. Based on this data 500 questionnaires are administered in all, taking a sample of 25 per cent of the businessmen. As the ratio of males to females in the entire Mandal is 3:2 of the 500 schedules, 300 are administered to male entrepreneurs and 200 to female entrepreneurs. These schedules are administered to Tribal and Non-tribal entrepreneurs in the ratio of their population in the Mandal, i.e., 4:1.

As the entrepreneurs of Paderu Mandal are scattered in all the 196 villages of the Mandal, 50 villages were selected at random and schedules were administered to the selected enetrepreneurs of the sample villages. While selecting the entrepreneurs due care is taken to cover those engaged in different types of trade to make the sample truly representative of the universe. The data gathered from the schedules are consolidated and tabulated.

**Economic Status of Entrepreneurs**

To know about the economic status of entrepreneurs, data relating to their annual incomes are gathered and the distribution of entrepreneurs on the basis of their level of income is presented in Table 21.1. It can be observed from Table 21.1 that a majority of the entrepreneurs (85.80 per cent) have an annual income of less than Rs.10,000, 10.40 per cent in the range of Rs. 10,000 Rs. 20,000, 3 per cent in the range of Rs. 20,000 Rs. 30,000 and less than one per cent with an annual income exceeding Rs. 30,000. In other words a majority of the entrepreneurs have a poor status. Among the entrepreneurs, the Tribals are poorer than Non-Tribals. This is evident from the fact that in lower income ranges, the percentage of Tribal entrepreneurs is far higher than that of Non-tribal entrepreneurs. For instance in the income range of less than Rs. 5,000, 91.88 per cent are Tribal entrepreneurs whereas only 8.12 per cent are Non-tribal entrepreneurs, and likewise in the income range of Rs. 5,000 to 10,000 while 70.23 per cent are Tribal entrepreneurs, only 29.77 per cent are Non-tribal entrepreneurs. The data however do not suggest that economic stauts of female entrepreneurs is lower or higher than that of male entrepreneurs.

It is observed that entrepreneurs in tribal areas have got other incomes too. Some of them work as agricultural labourers in certain seasons of the year and make some income, while some others have agricultural income in addition to income from their business enterprises. Consequently to know about the importance of business as a source of income, the percentage of their business income of total income is calculated and the entrepreneurs are classified on the basis of percentage of their business income of total income. The relevant data is presented in Table 21.2. It can be observed from Table 21.2 that for 71.40 per cent of the entrepreneurs, business income constitutes more than 75.00 per cent of their total income. For 16.00 per cent of the entrepreneurs, it constitutes 50-75 per cent of their total income and for 12.60 per cent of the entrepreneurs it constitutes less than 50.00 per cent of their total business income. It means that for a majority of the entrepreneurs, business income constitutes the chief or major source of income.

**Table 21.1**

**Paderu Mandal Distribution of Tribal and Non-Tribal Entrepreneurs on the Basis of their Annual Income**

| *Annual Income (In Rs.)* | *Tribals* | | | *Non-Tribals* | | | *Grand Total* |
|---|---|---|---|---|---|---|---|
| Less than | (75.84) | (84.38) | (79.25) | (20.00) | (40.00) | (28.00) | (69.00) |
| 5,000 | 182 | 135 | 317 | 12 | 16 | 28 | 345 |
| | (57.41) | (42.59) | (91.88) | (42.86) | (57.14) | (8.12) | (100.00) |
| 5,000– | (17.08) | (11.25) | (14.75) | (28.33) | (20.00) | (25.00) | (16.80) |
| 10,000 | 41 | 18 | 69 | 17 | 8 | 25 | 84 |
| | (69.49) | (30.51) | (70.23) | (68.00) | (32.00) | (29.77) | (100.00) |
| 10,000– | (4.17) | (3.12) | (3.75) | (41.67) | (30.00) | (37.00) | (10.40) |
| 20,000 | 10 | 5 | 15 | 25 | 12 | 37 | 52 |
| | (66.67) | (33.33) | (28.84) | (65.57) | (32.44) | (71.16) | (100.00) |
| 20,000– | (2.08) | (1.25) | (1.76) | (8.33) | (7.50) | (8.00) | (3.00) |
| 30,000 | 5 | 2 | 7 | 5 | 3 | 8 | 15 |
| | (71.43) | (28.57) | (46.66) | (62.50) | (37.50) | (53.34) | (100.00) |
| Above | (0.83) | — | (0.50) | (1.67) | (2.50) | (2.00) | (0.80) |
| 30,000 | 2 | | 2 | 1 | 1 | 2 | 4 |
| | (100.00) | | (50.00) | (50.00) | (50.00) | (50.00) | (100.00) |
| Total | 240 | 160 | 400 | 60 | 40 | 100 | 500 |

*Note :* Figures in brackets below the absolute numbers indicate percentages to horizontal total while those above them indicate percentages to vertical totals.

**Table 21.2**
**Paderu Mandal Distribution of Tribal and Non-Tribal Entrepreneurs on the Basis of Percentage of their Business Income to Total Income**

| *Per centage Share of business income to total income* | *Tribals* | | | *Non-Tribals* | | | *Grand Total* |
|---|---|---|---|---|---|---|---|
| | *Males* | *Females* | *Total* | *Males* | *Females* | *Total* | |
| Less than | (8.75) | (21.88) | (14.00) | (5.00) | (10.00) | (7.00) | (12.60) |
| 50 | 21 | 35 | 56 | 3 | 4 | 7 | 63 |
| | (37.50) | (62.50) | (88.89) | (42.86) | (57.14) | (11.11) | (100.00) |
| 50-75 | (19.58) | (15.00) | (17.75) | (8.33) | (10.00) | (9.00) | (16.00) |
| | 47 | 24 | 71 | 5 | 4 | 9 | 80 |
| | (66.20) | (33.80) | (88.75) | (55.56) | (44.44) | (11.25) | (100.00) |
| 75-100 | (71.67) | (63.12) | (68.25) | (86.67) | (80.00) | (84.00) | (71.40) |
| | 172 | 101 | 273 | 52 | 32 | 84 | 357 |
| | (63.00) | (37.00) | (76.47) | (61.90) | (38.10) | (23.53) | (100.00) |
| Total | 240 | 160 | 400 | 60 | 40 | 100 | 500 |

*Note:* Figures in brackets below the absolute numbers indicate percentages to horizontal totals, while those above them indicate percentages to vertical total.

## Occupational Mobility

A knowledge of the main occupations of the entrepreneurs prior to commencement of business would throw light on occupational mobility besides providing the background needed to elicit the reasons for their entry into business. With this end in view, data relating to the occupations of the entrepreneurs prior to commencement of business are gathered and distribution of entrepreneurs on this basis is presented in Table 21.3. It could be observed from Table 21.3 that though the entrepreneurs came from different occupations, a majority of them (59.80 per cent) were engaged in agriculture before commencing business. Inadequacy of income in those occupations, drove them into business. It is interesting to note in this connection, that the percentage of Non-tribal entrepreneurs with employment background (24.00 per cent) is far higher than that of Tribal entrepreneurs (0.75 per cent) with the same background. This shows that the former have greater occupational mobility than the latter. Further the percentage of female entrepreneurs both among Tribals and Non-Tribals, who switched over to business from vocations like collection of forest produce and collection of firewood is far higher than that of male entrepreneurs hailing from the same vocation. This reveals that females showed greater mobility than males to improve their income.

**Reasons for Entry into Business**

Data relating to distribution of entrepreneurs on the basis of reasons which favoured their entry into business, are provided in Table 21.4. It could be observed from Table 21.4 that a majority of the entrepreneurs (91.60 per cent) switched over to business due to inadequacy of incomes in their former occupations. Inability to secure jobs, and availability of help from friends and relatives are the other reasons for entry into business. That lack of jobs is not cited as a reason even by a single tribal female entrepreneur, indicates that the tribal female entrepreneurs are not qualified for securing a job nor did they try for it, before plunging into business.

When the entrepreneurs are asked about their participation in any entrepreneurial development programme, only ten of them (2.00 per cent) responded in the affirmative, all of whom happen to be non Tribals running small scale Industries in the Mandal. It is also mentioned that they attended a two months programme organised by a Commercial Bank, in the course of which principles and practices of running of enterprises were explained to them and that they found the programme useful. When Tribal and Non-tribal entrepreneurs, who have not attended any such programme were contacted, about 70.00 per cent of the Non-Tribal entrepreneurs informed that they did not consider it relevant or useful for the enterprises they were

**Table 21.3**
**Paderu Mandal Distribution of Tribal and Non-Tribal Entrepreneurs on the Basis of their Main Occupation before Commencing Business**

| *Item* | *Tribals* | | | *Non-Tribals* | | | *Grand Total* |
|---|---|---|---|---|---|---|---|
| | *Males* | *Females* | *Total* | *Males* | *Females* | *Total* | |
| Agriculture | (66.66) | (51.25) | (60.50) | (53.34) | (62.50) | (87.00) | (59.80) |
| | 160 | 82 | 242 | 32 | 25 | 57 | 299 |
| | (66.12) | (33.88) | (80.94) | (56.14) | (43.86) | (19.06) | (100.00) |
| Agricultu- | (20.84) | (22.50) | (21.50) | (13.33) | (20.00) | (16.00) | (20.40) |
| ral Labour | 50 | 36 | 86 | 8 | 8 | 16 | 102 |
| | (58.14) | (41.86) | (84.31) | (50.00) | (50.00) | (15.69) | (100.00) |
| Collection | (5.00) | (13.75) | (8.50) | — | (2.50) | (1.00) | (7.00) |
| of Forest | 12 | 22 | 34 | | 1 | 1 | 35 |
| Produce | (35.29) | (64.71) | (97.14) | | (100.00) | (2.86) | (100.00) |
| Collection | (5.42) | (12.50) | (8.25) | — | (2.50) | (1.00) | (7.00) |
| of Fire- | 13 | 20 | 33 | | 2 | 2 | 35 |
| wood | (39.39) | (60.61) | (94.28) | | (100.00) | (5.72) | (100.00) |
| Hunting | (0.83) | — | (0.50) | — | — | — | (100.00) |
| | 2 | | 2 | | | | 2 |
| | (100.00) | | (100.00) | | | | (100.00) |
| Employ- | (1.25) | — | (0.75) | (33.33) | (0.00) | (24.00) | (5.40) |
| ment | 3 | | 3 | 20 | 4 | 24 | 27 |
| | (100.00) | | (11.11) | (83.33) | (16.67) | (88.89) | (100.00) |
| Total | 240 | 160 | 400 | 60 | 40 | 100 | 500 |

*Note:* Figures in brackets below the absolute numbers indicate percentages to horizontal totals, while those above them indicate percentages to vertical totals.

**Table 21.4**
**Paderu Mandal Distribution of Tribal and Non-Tribal Entrepreneurs on the Basis of Reasons Behind their Entry into Business**

| *Reason behind entry into business* | *Tribals* | | | *Non-Tribals* | | | *Grand Total* |
|---|---|---|---|---|---|---|---|
| | *Males* | *Females* | *Total* | *Males* | *Females* | *Total* | |
| Inadequacy | (95.83) | (93.75) | (95.00) | (80.00) | (75.00) | (78.00) | (91.60) |
| of income | 230 | 150 | 380 | 48 | 30 | 78 | 458 |
| from earlier occupation | (60.53) | (39.471) | (82.97 | (61.54) | (38.46) | (17.03) | (100.00) |
| Lack of Jobs | (1.25) | — | (0.75) | (16.67) | (20.00) | (18.00) | (4.20) |
| | 3 | | 3 | 10 | 8 | 18 | 21 |
| | (100.00) | | (14.28) | (55.55) | (44.45) | (85.72) | (100.00) |
| Availability | (2.92) | (6.25) | (4.25) | (3.33) | (5.00) | (4.00) | (4.20) |
| of help from | 7 | 10 | 17 | 2 | 2 | 4 | 21 |
| friends and relatives | (41.18) | (58.82) | (80.95) | (50.00) | (50.00) | (19.05) | (100.00) |
| Total | 240 | 160 | 400 | 60 | 40 | 100 | 500 |

*Note:* Figures in brackets below the absolute numbers indicate percentages to horizontal totals, while those above them indicate to vertical totals.

running. While the other 30.00 per cent of Non-tribals and almost all the Tribal entrepreneurs informed that they were not aware of any such programme. This calls for organising entrepreneurial develop-ment programmes with a view to developing skills needed by the entrepreneurs and for giving wide publicity to ensure adequate participation.

**Problems Faced by the Entrepreneurs**

The entrepreneurs both Tribals and Non-Tribals are facing many problems such as injustice at the hands of Girijan Corporation, procurement of funds from money-lenders at high rates of interest, local competition, transport bottlenecks, etc. These are dealt within the following paragraphs.

1. The manner of raising the funds needed for investment in business would also have a bearing on the success of the business, because if funds are borrowed at high rate of interest, interest commitments prove burdensome and upset the profits that would have otherwise accrued to the entrepreneurs. As such data pertaining the sources from which funds are raised by the entrepreneurs for investment in the business, was gathered and the same is presented in Table 21.5. It can be observed from Table 21.5 that a majority of them (55.20 per cent) raised the funds by way of borrowings from money lenders, that too at high rates of interest ranging from 30.00 per cent to 60.00 per cent per annum. 22.00 per cent invested their own funds, 8.20 per cent raised funds from Government agencies, 7.40 per cent from banks and 7.20 per cent from friends and relatives. When asked about the reason for approaching money-lenders, they indicated that they were not able to secure loans from banks or other agencies as the bankers insisted, on land documents as a security, which most of them did not possess.

This shows that interest commitments prove burdensome to a majority of the entrepreneurs and depress the profits that would have otherwise accrued to them. Hence it is necessary that the entrepreneurs approach the banks or other Government Agencies for securing funds for investment in business. It could be further observed from Table 21.5 that the percentage of female entrepreneurs securing funds from own capital, friends and relatives and banks is higher than that of male entrepreneurs in the Tribals category, which means that Tribal females are able to avoid recourse to money lenders by tapping other sources available to them. In the same way, the percentage of male entrepreneurs in the Non-Tribals category securing funds from own capital, friends and relatives, and banks is higher than that of female entrepreneurs, which means that male Non-Tribal Entrepreneurs are able to raise funds mostly from agencies other than money lenders.

**Table 21.5**
**Paderu Mandal—Classification of Tribal and Non-Tribal Entrepreneurs on the Basis of Sources of Funds for Investment**

| *Sources of Funds of Investment* | *Tribals* | | | *Non-Tribals* | | | *Grand Total* |
|---|---|---|---|---|---|---|---|
| | *Males* | *Females* | *Total* | *Males* | *Females* | *Total* | |
| Own Capital | (8.33) | (18.75) | (12.50) | (53.33) | (70.00) | (60.00) | (22.00) |
| | 20 | 30 | 50 | 32 | 28 | 60 | 110 |
| | (40.00) | (60.00) | (45.45) | (53.33) | (46.67) | (54.55) | (100.00) |
| Friends | (2.50) | (12.50) | (6.50) | (8.33) | (12.50) | (10.00) | (7.20) |
| and | 6 | 20 | 26 | 5 | 5 | 10 | 36 |
| Relatives | (23.08) | (76.92) | (72.22) | (50.00) | (50.00) | (22.78) | (100.00) |
| Money | (75.00) | (52.50) | (66.00) | (8.33) | (17.50) | (12.00) | (55.20) |
| Lenders | 180 | 84 | 264 | 5 | 7 | 12 | 276 |
| | (68.18) | (31.82) | (95.65) | (41.67) | (58.33) | (4.35) | (100.00) |
| Banks | (3.75) | (6.25) | (4.75) | (30.00) | — | (18.00) | (7.40) |
| | 9 | 10 | 19 | 18 | | 18 | 37 |
| | (47.37) | (52.63) | (51.35) | (100.00) | | (48.65) | (100.00) |
| Government | (10.42) | (10.00) | (10.25) | — | — | — | (8.20) |
| Agencies | 25 | 16 | 41 | | | | 41 |
| | (60.98) | (39.02) | (100.00) | | | | (100.00) |
| Total | 240 | 160 | 400 | 60 | 40 | 100 | 500 |

*Note:* Figures in brackets below the absolute numbers indicate percentages to horizontal totals, while those above them indicate percentages to vertical totals.

2. Interaction with the entrepreneurs reveals that those who are selling directly to the customers are not facing any problems, but those selling to the Girijan Coop. Corporation are facing many problems. The problems faced by the entrepreneurs were

ascertained and the relevant data is presented in Table 21.6. It may be observed from Table 21.6 that delayed payments, deceit by the officials, manipulation of weighment and measurement by Shandy Inspectors, cumbersomeness of procedure are some of the problems faced by the entrepreneurs selling goods directly to the Girijan Co-op. Corporation.

3. Distribution of entrepreneurs on the basis of type of problems faced is shown in Table 21.7. It can be observed from Table 21.7 that a majority of the entrepreneurs (73.40 per cent) complain that they are not able to get financial assistance from banks, 17.40 per cent complain that interest commitments are proving burdensome. 7.60 per cent complain of growing competition in the already limited local markets and 1.60 per cent complain of transport bottlenecks due to inadequacy of transport facilities.

**Suggestions**

1. An examination of the manner in which funds are raised by the entrepreneurs, reveals that a majority of them (55.20 per cent) raised the funds by way of borrowings from money lenders and only 7.40 per cent from banks. It is also observed that due to high rates of interest charged by money lenders, their profits are getting depressed. As such there is a need for providing institutional credit, that too at cheaper rates to the entrepreneurs of Tribal areas. Further possession of land documents should not be insisted upon for the purpose of granting loans at least in the case of Tribals.

2. Those who are selling their goods to the Girijan Corporation are facing some problems such as delayed payments, manipulation of weighment and measurement, deceit by officials, etc. Higher officials of the Corporation should exercise strict vigil over the field staff and initiate steps to cleanse the corporation particularly at lower levels.

3. Though the Integrated Tribal Development Agency constructed shopping complexes at certain places, they are constructed at places far off from places where Tribals habitually congregate to do their business, resulting in idleness of shopping complexes. Hence it is suggested that shopping complexes have to be constructed at places where Tribals congregate for doing business to make the scheme of shopping complexes successful.

**Table 21.6**
**Paderul Mandal—Problems Faced by the Tribal and Non-Tribal Entrepreneurs with the Girijan Co-operative Corporation**

| *Nature of Problem* | *Tribals* | | | *Non-Tribals* | | | *Grand Total* |
|---|---|---|---|---|---|---|---|
| | *Males* | *Females* | *Total* | *Males* | *Females* | *Total* | |
| Delayed | (22.72) | (53.84) | (36.44) | — | (33.34) | 33.33) | (38.29) |
| Payment | 15 | 28 | 43 | | 2 | 2 | 45 |
| | (34.88) | (65.12) | (95.56) | | (100.00) | (4.44) | (100.00) |
| Deceit by | (42.42) | (23.08) | (33.90) | — | (33.34) | (33.33) | (33.88) |
| officials | 28 | 12 | 40 | | 2 | 2 | 42 |
| | (70.00) | (30.00) | (95.24) | | (100.00) | (4.76) | (100.00) |
| Manipu- | (13.64) | (15.38) | (14.40) | — | (16.66) | (16.67) | (14.52 |
| lation of | 9 | 8 | 17 | | 1 | 1 | 18 |
| weighment measurement by Shandy Inspectors | (52.94 | (47.06) | (94.44) | | (100.00) | (5.56) | (100.00) |
| Non- | (18.19) | (3.84) | (11.86) | — | (16.66) | (16.67) | (12.09) |
| collection | 12 | 2 | 14 | | 1 | 1 | 15 |
| of Produce at doorstep | (85.71) | (14.29) | (93.33) | | (100.00) | (6.67) | (100.00) |
| Cumber- | (3.03) | (3.84) | (3.39) | — | — | — | (3.22) |
| someness of | 2 | 2 | 4 | | | | 4 |
| procedure | (50.00) | (50.00) | (100.00) | | | | (100.00) |
| Total | 66 | 52 | 118 | — | 6 | 6 | 124 |

*Note:* Figures in brackets below the absolute numbers indicate percentages to horizontal totals while those above them indicate percentages to the number of people selling to the Girijan Co-operative Corporation.

**Table 21.7**
**Paderu Mandal—Distribution of Tribal and Non-Tribal Entrepreneurs on the Basis of Types of Problem Faced**

| *Type of Problem faced* | *Tribals* | | | *Non-Tribals* | | | *Grand Total* |
|---|---|---|---|---|---|---|---|
| | *Males* | *Females* | *Total* | *Males* | *Females* | *Total* | |
| Competition | (9.17) | (5.62) | (7.75) | (8.33) | (5.00) | (7.00) | (7.60) |
| | 22 | 9 | 31 | 5 | 2 | 7 | 38 |
| | (70.97) | (29.03) | (81.58) | (71.43) | (28.57) | (18.42) | (100.00) |
| High Rates | (15.83) | (16.25) | (16.00) | (25.00) | (20.00) | (23.00) | (17.40) |
| of interest | 38 | 26 | 64 | 15 | 8 | 23 | 87 |
| | (59.38) | (40.62) | (73.56) | (65.22) | (34.78) | (26.44) | (100.00) |
| Transport | — | — | — | (10.00) | (5.00) | (8.00) | (1.60) |
| Bottlenecks | | | | 6 | 2 | 8 | 8 |
| | | | | (75.00) | (25.00) | (100.00) | (100.00) |
| Meagre | (75.00) | (78.13) | (76.25) | (56.67) | (70.00) | (62.00) | (73.40) |
| Assistance | 180 | 125 | 305 | 34 | 28 | 62 | 367 |
| from Banks | (59.02) | (40.98) | (83.11) | (54.84) | (45.16) | (16.89) | (100.00) |
| Fall in demand | — | — | — | — | — | — | — |
| Total | 240 | 160 | 400 | 60 | 40 | 100 | 500 |

*Note:* Figures in brackets below the absolute numbers indicate percentages to horizontal totals, while those above them indicate percentages to vertical totals.

## References

1. Among others John. W. Kondrick, "Production Trends in the United States," NBER 1961 Domar *et al.*, "Economic Growth and Productivity in the United States, Canada, United Kingdom,

Germany and Japan in the Post-war period", *The Review of Economics and Statistics*, Vol. XIVI, No. 1, Feb. 1964.

2. Sarveswara Rao, B. *et al.*, "Report on Commercial and Industrial Entrepreneurship in the Coastal Region of A.P.", ICSSR, Profit, New Delhi, 1979, p. 1.

# 22

# Role of Commercial Banks in Economic Development

—*V. Surya Rao*
—*K. Srinivasa Rao*

Entrepreneurship is the name given to the factor of production, which performs the function of "Enterprise". Out of the four factors of production, i.e., Land, Labour, Capital, Organisation and Enterprise, economic development of any country depends mainly upon initiative and enterprise. Resources are of no use unless there are entrepreneurs with constructive ability to take the fullest advantage of economic resources. India is quite rich in natural resources; we have good and cheap labour and a wide market too. One has to exploit these resources and opportunities in a planned way, to make India a very strong country. Entrepreneurs with constructive ability are needed to come forward and lead the nation. Interestingly, all the business enterprises require huge capital and unfortunately it is short in this country. We have therefore to look after the enterprise capital requirements, commercial banking network having to play a very important role in it. Without adequate finance, organisations cannot run smooth. One of the major objectives of nationalisation of banks, was to direct larger volumes of the banking sector into the important sector's like small scale industries, small traders, artisans, self-employed persons, etc.

The commercial banks, particularly after nationalisation, have been playing a key role in the economic and social transformation and development of our country. These banks have expanded incredibly fast in respect of number of branches as well as in diversifying its services in many directions. Apart from discharging their economic functions, the banks are entrusted with the challenging task of responding to certain social problems. Through their schemes, banks are catering to the needs of retail traders, rural artisans, village craftsmen, small businessmen, transport operators and self employed.

## Role of Banks in Economic Development

Distinguished economists in the past and present have very well deliberated the role of the banks in the process of economic development. A journey through the history of economics though shows what while this role of banks has been described and understood in various ways, over different periods, the following four roles stand out:

1. Banks as financial intermediaries,
2. The direct correlation between economic growth on the one hand and financial growth driven by the dynamism of the financial sector in general, and banks in particular, on the other.
3. The important role of banks in creation of money, which creates the demand for goods and services.
4. The role of banks as a catalyst of social development.
5. The role played by banks in facilitating promotion of entrepreneurship an essential condition of economic development.

I would like to stress on the role played by commercial banks in promotion of entrepreneurial activity which, further leads to economic development of the nation.

## Banks as Agents for Social Change in Developing Economies

For rapid economic development, it is necessary that all segments of the populace should be brought into the economic mainstream. Particularly, in case of a developing nation like India, which has a significant percentage of people living below the poverty line, banks should bring social change by broad-basing the economic growth.

There is no doubt to say that banks are the agents of social change. The special schemes adopted by banking system in India for weaker sections of society, such as Differential Interest Rate Scheme, Integrated Rural Development Programme, Prime Minister Rojgar Yojna and the special schemes for relatively isolated segments of society like tribals have had considerable impact in changing the shape of rural economy in India.

**Role of Commercial Banks in Promotion of Entrepreneurship**

The quality most needed for economic growth of a country is entrepreneurship, which means the capability to take risks in new venture. The spirit of entrepreneurship can find sustenance only in a society, which has a developed financial system. The financial system ensures that the capital, which is one of the most important sources for the entrepreneur is readily made available to him. In developing economies like India, where established entrepreneurs are few in number, the banks have to play a very important role in development of entrepreneurship. For this reason, the banks take special interest in creating conditions for development of entrepreneurship.

Financing schemes of banks and its capital assets alone would not bring about the much needed economic progress, promotional and developmental functions are equally important to banking institutions as the financing role. Over the period, commercial banks have evolved several comprehensive programmes for entrepreneurship development with a purpose to motivate first generation entrepreneurs to set up risk bearing ventures especially in industrially backward areas of the country.

The Entrepreneurship Development Programmes conducted by the banks are more or less similar in nature. The basic features of the EDPs are summed as:

1. Identification and careful selection of entrepreneurs for training;
2. Development of the entrepreneurial capabilities of the trainees;
3. Equipping the trainees with basic managerial understanding;
4. Ensuring a viable industrial project for each potential entrepreneur; and
5. Helping him to secure necessary financial and related

assistance.

However, the main functional area through which banks can help development of entrepreneurship is the deployment of credit. The following are the schemes relating to small scale industries, traders, small business entrepreneurs and professionals.

**(A) Schemes Relating to Small Scale Industries**

1. *Credit to Small Scale Industries:* Small Scale units can avail term loan facilities for acquisition of machinery to a maximum amount of 50 per cent of the cost for a period of 5 to 7 years. Besides, they provide working capital loans. The working capital loan is disbursed in the form of overdraft, cash credit, etc.
2. *Financing the Establishment of Small-Scale Units by Technician Entrepreneurs:* Under this scheme, Bank provides a term loan of Rs. 5 lakhs to the technician entrepreneurs for establishing an industrial unit.
3. *Financing and Development of Khadi and Village Industries Under KVIC Interest:* Under this scheme, a bank grants a working capital loan up to a maximum amount of Rs. 1500 to a borrower covered under the KVIC interest subsidy scheme at an interest rate equal to 4 per cent above the bank rate, out of which 4 per cent will be recovered from the borrower and the remaining interest from the KVIC in the form of subsidy interest. This facility is open to a borrower whose family income from all sources does not exceed Rs. 3000 per annum, and he should not own in excess of one acre of irrigated land.
4. *Finance to Tiny Sector of SSI:* Banks provide term loans as well as working capital loans to borrowers covered under the tiny sector at an interest rate of 9.5 per cent for borrowers in backward areas and 11 per cent for those in other areas.

**(B) Schemes Relating to Traders and Small Business Entrepreneurs**

Traders can get finance from banks to satisfy their working capital needs as well as for the purchase of any equipment. Term loans can be obtained against hypothecation.

Traders dealing in fertilisers can obtain working capital loans subject to the condition that the borrower continues to have authorised dealership.

Small Business Enterprises can avail finance from commercial banks to satisfy their working capital requirements as well as term loan for purchase of any equipment. Equipment finance can be obtained up to a maximum limit of Rs. 50,000 and is to be payable in 36 monthly instalments.

### *(C) Schemes Relating to Self-Employed and Professionals*

Banks provide credit facilities to engineers, technicians, architects and other self employed persons and professionals to enable them to meet medium term as well as short term financial needs. Usually the monthly instalments may be lower in the initial stage and then raised gradually. To avail this facility, the applicant must have minimum 5 years of experience in the line and should have had a justifiable income.

## Entrepreneurial Assistance by Banks

1. *Entrepreneurial Banking:* This scheme has been started by Bank of Baroda in collaboration with Uttar Pradesh Small Industries Corporation to assist techno-entrepreneurs to set up units. Under this scheme, assistance will be provided to the technician for acquisition of fixed assets and current assets and also these technicians are provided in plant training in established units.
2. *Entrepreneurial Clinics:* This is a scheme from Bank of India. Under this scheme, a panel of industrialists will adopt budding entrepreneurs to guide and assist them.
3. *Indian Bank Entrepreneur Advisory Service:* The bank provides consultancy services to persons who graduate from colleges and institutions of engineering technology, etc., and unemplo-yed engineers, diploma holders and other graduates or business executives. Consultancy would be provided right from the beginning of identification of project to its implementation and marketing. For this purpose a cell has been established comprising of bank employees and selected experts.

In addition to these, Grindlays Bank has established two divisions, i.e., Small Scale Consultancy Services and Merchant Banking Division. The former offers services relating to project feasibility. The Merchant Banking Division manages public issues for raising capital, helps establish liaison with government lending bodies for raising long term development finance.

**Concluding Remarks**

During the pre-independence period, financial constraints had hampered the rapid development of industries. After independence, the government has built up a strong financial system to provide financial support to all types of industries. Towards this end, banks have shouldered responsibility of development of industry and entrepreneurship. In fact, this area does not come strictly within the purview of the role of Commercial Banks.

In this context, there are few points to be borne in mind. First, after nationalisation banks have identified themselves with policies of government in the matters of enterprise promotion. Second, Banks interest rate structure is generally graded on slab basis, with a favourable bias towards the priority sectors.

Banks are not just financing capital requirements of the industry, but stimulating entrepreneurial activity by providing management consultancy, developing new skills and creating the much needed entrepreneurial awareness.

# 23

# Role of Women Entrepreneurship in Economic Development

—*Dr. S. Rajani*

"Entrepreneurship is the key to rapid economic development". This statement has been found to be true in a number of cases. Growth of capital is no longer considered as important as the growth of innovative manpower, such as the entrepreneurs, in the determination of the rate of economic development of a nation. Entrepreneurship is the vehicle which mobilizes the scarce resources from different sectors and provides utility to them such that they create value. The experiences of several prosperous countries indicates that entrepreneurship is the magic wand which creates miracles of prosperity.

The role of entrepreneurship in economic development is not unknown to us because the former has been playing a significant role in the development of business in India from the days of Indus Valley Civilisation when our merchants were always ready with new products, entering new markets. With the gradual transformation of the society over the years, the economic scenario has also undergone a sea-change. Intensified competition has become the order of the day and entrepreneurship is cited by many social scientists as the key variable which links the socio-cultural milieu with the rate of economic development.

In earlier days the rate of entrepreneurial participation was dependent on a number of socio-cultural factors like caste, size of the family, econimic status, level of education, training, etc. For example *e.g.*, the entrepreneurial activity was influenced significantly by the family. The Indian extended family with its ability to mobilize large resources, facilitated the acquisition of entrepreneurial training and the establishment of firms; at the same time joint family in India also curtailed the expansion of firms by diverting the resources for current consumption which might otherwise have been reinvested in the business. However, with the government having acknowledged the significance of entrepreneurship and taking an active part in creating a conducive environment for entrepreneurship trading, the scenario has changed a lot.

According to Joseph Schumpeter, the rate of economic progress of a nation depends upon the rate of innovation which in turn depends upon the distribution of entrepreneurial talent in the population. Technical progress alone cannot lead to economic development, unless technological breakthroughs are put to economic use by entrepreneurs. In other words an entrepreneur acts as a catalyst in the process of industrialisation and economic development. How do they accomplish this? Entrepreneurs mobilise idle savings of the public and help in capital formation, locate and convert the latent and idle resources into national income and wealth; generate employment both directly as well as indirectly; contribute to improvement in the living standards; facilitate establishment of forward and backward linkages.

However, entrepreneurial development in the country is still plagued by a number of problems like the absence of a concerted effort for entrepreneurship development. Managerial skills in terms of acquisition and allocation of resources and handling crisis situations are most often lacking in the current breed of Indian entrepreneurs. In spite of the existence of a large number of institutions like District Industries Centres, State Financial Corporations, SIDBI (Small Industries Development Bank of India), Entrepreneurship Development Institutes, etc., first generation entrepreneurs are finding it difficult to survive and grow in their chosen business.

Another important facet of entrepreneurship in India is the emergence of a large number of women entrepreneurs. Earlier the involvement of women in the establishment and management of business enterprises was very limited/negligible because as in the case of most of the developing countries, in India too, women have been victim of social prejudice and discrimination. They were presumed to be the weak, passive, dependent and people-oriented. However, during the past 2-3 decades Indian women have made their mark in different walks of like, thanks to the increased levels of education, political awakening, urbanisation, legal safeguards, social reforms, etc. It has been proved in several instances that business is the best occupation for women since it gives them a chance to apply their creativity, earn additional income for the family, maintain self-respect, flexibility of working hours, etc. Compared to the developed countries, women entrepreneurs constitute a negligible proportion of the total entrepreneurs in India. Earlier they were running mostly household industries like pickles, pappads, powders, detergents, etc. These are being gradually replaced by more sophisticated and capital intensive enterprises like textiles, machinery, electronics, engineering goods, etc.

Entrepreneurship serve as a boon for rural women in countries like India where the rural women find it difficult to make both ends meet with the meagre earnings of their male counterparts. Their illiteracy and ignorance prevents them from being gainfully employed. Therefore, if they are encouraged to start their own cottage enterprises with minimum stake it would help in making them self-sufficient and even contribute their might to the overall economic development of the country. A recent survey conducted in Visakhapatnam district by the writer revealed that even in some of the remote tribal mandals of Visakhapatnam district women were found to be enthusiastic in starting their own ventures. With support from Government agencies and voluntary organisations through programmes aimed at integrated rural development, a substantial number of women entrepreneurs have come forward and are successfully running a wide variety of enterprises like toy making units, basket making, primary schools, handicrafts, etc. In semi-urban and urban areas women are running beauty parlours, fitness centres, boutiques, small shops, rice mills, etc. With a few operating in more sophisticated fields like engineering, machinery, electronics, fashion jewellery, etc., also.

The government has been providing a lot of support in the

form of financial, technical, infrastructural and training facilities. National Institute of Entrepreneurship and Small Business Development (NIESBUD), New Delhi, plays an active role in designing and implementing training and research facilities in entrepreneurship. There are several other schemes like the Integrated Rural Development Programmes (IRDP), Self Employment Schemes for Educated Unemployed Youth (SESEUY), Self Employment Programme for Urban Poor (SEPUP), National Rural Employment Programme (NREP), etc. which encourage women and rural entrepreneurs.

Women entrepreneurs face special problems and constraints in India like illiteracy/low level of literacy, not having access to vital and timely information, being risk-averse, feeling of insecurity, lack of experience, etc.

Some of the problems stated by women entrepreneurs in Visakhapatnam district are—

*Low Level of Education*—Literacy among women is found to be very low. In the urban areas more number of women receive education but not professional or techinical education, as a result of which when women wish to start their own enterprise, they face difficulties in gathering information about various aspects of business like technological upgradation, marketing support from government, managing financial resources, etc. This prevents them from entering more profitable and non-conventional areas.

*Financial Constraints*—Like any small/new entrepreneur, availability of adequate funds is a major constraint for women entrepreneurs. However, in the case of women it is more pronounced because in most of the cases they do not have any property in their name which can be sold or offered as tangible security for securing credit in the money market. Banks are often sceptical about the seriousness of the women entrepreneurs; moreover, the complicated procedures and delay involved in obtaining bank loans often deters women entrepreneurs from approaching them for help to meet their investment and working capital requirements.

*Problems of Marketing*—The biggest handicap for women entrepreneurs is lack of mobility which forces them to approach middlemen to arrange for the sale for their goods/services who try to exploit them. This also prevents them from expanding their markets since they are not in direct contact with the market and are unaware of the opportunities and threats in the market.

*Family Responsibilities*—In India women have greater responsibility towards the family, and hence depend heavily on the encouragement and co-operation from her family members. Her active involvement in family leaves little energy and time for business, wherein actually business requires a lot of attention and is much different from the traditional 9 a.m. to 5 p.m. jobs. It requires total involvement on the part of the entrepreneur to be able to take timely decisions and their effective implementation. The demanding nature of her dual roles creates a lot of pressure and most of the women entrepreneurs find it difficult to cope up with this pressure.

*Social Attitudes*—Though our constitution provides for equality and encourages women empowerment, there is a lot of gender-based discrimination in our society. This is more prominent in the rural areas wherein a female child is often considered as a liability to be got rid of as early as possible and hence investment on girls education or training is generally considered a waste. They are rather allowed to be helpers than being encouraged to start their own enterprises.

Lack of self-confidence, low risk bearing nature, unplanned growth, late start, lack of infrastructure, suppressed need for achievement, lack of independence and autonomy, etc., are some of the other problems exclusive to women entrepreneurs in India.

It is very heartening to observe that a number of government and voluntary organisations have been offering support to women entrepreneurs to help them overcome their teething problems and successfully manage their enterprises. Adequate importance has been given to the development of women entrepreneurs in the successive economic plans from the Seventh Five Year Plan onwards. The plan allocations have been mostly used to provide infrastructural, marketing and training facilities besides creating awareness on need to encourage women entrepreneurship and enact legislation to remove constraints in their way. The National Alliance of Young Entrepreneurs (NAYE) has been doing commendable work in this area.

Several international agencies like UNCTAD, UNDP, ILO, etc., have been initiating fiscal and financial measures to encourage women entrepreneurs across the globe and help them participate in international trade. There are a few organisations which are exclusively towards the development of women entrepreneur-ship in the country, viz., Women entrepreneur wing of NAYE, Indian Council of Women Entrepreneurs, Federation of Indian Chambers of Commerce & Industry (FICCI), Ladies Organisations, National Commission on Self Employed Women in the Informal sector, World Association of Women Entreprenurs (WAWE), Associated Country Women of the World (ACWW), etc.

In spite of all these efforts it is observed that the rate of growth of entrepreneurial activity among women in the country is still limited and not as much as desired. The institution of a central body to co-ordinate the scattered efforts in this area is essential. There is an urgent need for reorientation of educational system for women, career guidance, change of curriculum, timely assistance, etc., for which there must be a close intergration among the efforts of the various organisations working with this objective. Reservations and appropriate concessions need to be offered to women entrepreneurs which are easily accessible.

# 24

# Entrepreneur Development Education and Training: A Global Perspective

—*Dr. S. Arumugam*

## Introduction

Educational institutions are engaged in human resource. development. Traditionally they have been developing employees. Because of industrialization and privatisation, creation of employers, that is entrepreneurs, has become important. The educational system is new to this area of human resource development. Formal education in this area began in 1970s (Scott 1995). Currently education is available up to doctoral level (Meredith 1996). In this Chapter an attempt has been made to describe the type of education and training programmes offered by various countries of the world. Details are given about the activities going on in USA, India and China which are operating at three distinct levels of entrepreneur development. Data has been collected from publications of 1990s. The information given in this Chapter will be very useful to people and organisations involved in entrepreneur development.

## Role of the Government in Development of Entrepreneurs

Entrepreneurs are required to create organisations and develop them. Organisations provide goods, services and employment to people. The government is the co-ordinator of the resources of the country. One of the important expectation of its people from the government is the effective management of production and supply of goods and services combined with employment. Depending upon the government philosophy, the production and distribution of goods and services are in the hands of government or transferred to private sector. As long as the government is directly involved in production and distribution, the question of entrepreneur development does not assume significance because the government plays the role of the entrepreneur. When the government wants to transfer this function to the private ownership then the government has to identify people and transfer this job to them.

Generally the government starts with policies to develop industries, not entrepreneurs. This is true in most of the countries. They realised the importance of entrepreneur development only when their attempt to industrialize faced problems regarding the availability of competent persons to start and develop new industries. This made the governments to go for promoting entrepreneur development (TANSTIA 1991).

Industries are created in three levels—large, medium and small. There is a relationship between the nature of ownership and the size of the industry. The governments are faced with the problem of giving preference in terms of developing large or small industries. Large industries are created by existing business houses or multinationals as per the recent trends. The promoters of large industries and multinationals are successful entrepreneurs. Such people are not interested in starting small industries. Hence the government has to identify people who are interested in starting small enterprises. Identification is not the end of the problem solving. Such individuals should be educated and trained to start industries. At this point in time the government has to turn to the educational institutions to help the government in development of entrepreneurs.

**Role of Educational Institutions in Entrepreneur Development**

The institutions started with training programmes. The target groups are unemployed and those who wanted to become entrepreneurs. The training feedback gave them further directions in entrepreneur development. Courses were offered as part of under-graduate and post-graduate programmes. Then the scenario shifted from universities and colleges to schools. The courses offered provided them the required knowledge of entrepreneurship. The training programmes helped in specific skill development. Science and technology entrepreneurs parks provided the entrepreneurs with facilities to start industries. Databank, library and research provided additional information and new directions for the development of entrepreneurs. National and international conferences, workshops and seminars are organised to share experiences in this area. Some departments, particularly management departments, in educational institutions, have taken leading role in this area because of the type of input provided by these departments which are vital for entrepreneur development. Many centres were established for entrepreneur development education, research and training. Several training models have been proposed. The models proposed are appropriately used. The important influencing factors of this entrepreneur development is the culture and the political philosophy of the particular country.

**Leaders, Learners, Laggards in Entrepreneur Development**

Those countries privatized early are the leaders in entrepreneur development. The example of such a country is USA. The countries which practiced mixed economy and started privatising industrial activity are relatively knowledgeable in this area. The example of such a country is India. Such of those countries where industries were completely operated by the government and started going for privatization have begun to learn entrepreneur development. An example of such a country is China. Thus, the various countries of the world can be grouped into three categories with respect to the expertise in entrepreneur development as leaders, learners and laggards. About fifty countries of the world are visible in the world of entrepreneurship development.

**Leader in Entrepreneur Development**

In the countries classified as leaders, entrepreneurship is a career option. Hence education is available at schools, colleges and Universities. There is no question of testing competencies. Competencies are acquired through education and training.

Among the countries who can be considered as leaders, USA is taken for discussion to highlight the various education and training activities in the area of entrepreneur development. The type of inputs available through the business schools for entrepreneur developemnt in USA (Katherine and Michael 1995) are:

1. Sizing up entrepreneurial opportunities
2. Analysis of business risks
3. Raising capital
4. Finding customers
5. Survival strategies of business
6. Launching and marketing products
7. Operational management/manufacturing techniques
8. Managing people
9. Exit strategies
10. Pricing strategies
11. Exploiting global opportunities
12. Transfer of technology
13. Commercialization of innovation.

Some of the students who have succeeded in business have the following to say about the education and training they had at the business schools. The points are:

1. Business school experience is a viable means to launch an entrepreneurial career.
2. Business schools are incredibly useful through the information resources, the management courses, the brainstorming and networking.
3. People without MBA start run successful business but it is a risk.
4. How to have a thick skin and say nothing offends me any more?

The comments of the teachers who teach the skills and attitudes that create success in business have the following to say:

1. We can't make people into entrepreneurs if they don't have the basic drive, energy and strong sense of what it takes to run a business. Students with these basic skills can be made much better entrepreneurs.

2. Successful entrepreneurs are by necessity and natural inclination superior learners and superior teachers and they do this every day.
3. In 1970s we knew very little about venture capital or where the money came from. But today we can be very precise. There in no other paradigm in the management sciences about which we have learned so much in so little time. We have come a long way but not far enough.
4. A large fraction of people who say "I am going to be an entrepreneur" are not.

With the change in the job market in the corporate sector, particularly with respect to security of job, students are considering entrepreneurship as the rewarding option to jobs. The demand for the entrepreneurial education in business schools are increasing. Some of the significant changes which are taking place in entrepreneurial education in business schools (Lord and Westfall 1996) are:

1. The best and brightest who specialize in consulting and investment banking now want to be entrepreneurs.
2. The percentage of students who express their interest to start business and launch their business after earning their degree, increases.
3. Courses in entrepreneurship have increased.
4. More funds are given to expand entrepreneurship programmes.
5. Corporations are pitching entrepreneurial opportunities to enterprising MBA's.
6. Most of the MBA's from Harvard went to large corporations and then to entrepreneurship. About 40 per cent students who graduated in 1974 from Harvard Business School are entrepreneurs today.

**Learner in Entrepreneur Development**

In India entrepreneur development activities have been started by industries development organisations. The training programmes started in 1970s. The pioneering institutions are National Institute of Small Industry Extension Training and Centre for Entrepreneurship Development, Gujarat. In the later years, National Institute of Entrepreneurship and Small Business

Development, Entrepreneurship Development Institute of India, Technical Consultancy Organisations, Entrepreneurship Development Cells, Science and Technology Entrepreneurs Parks, District Industries Centres, Industries Associations have started the entrepreneur development training. An estimate in the year 1995 indicates that about 600 organisations are involved in entrepreneur development training (Prem 1995).

Introduction of Entrepreneurship Development Education also began in 1970s. Indian Institute of Management, Ahmedabad offers courses in Entrepreneurship Development since 1970. The IIT Madras introduced M.S. in Entrepreneurship Development in 1983. At the initiative of the National Science and Technology Entepreneurship Development Board, Ashoka Chandra Committee gave the syllabus for entrepreneurship development for adoption in Engineering Colleges in the year 1985. In the late 1980s science and technology institutions introduced entrepreneurship development courses in engineering and technology programmes.

The experience of Indian Institute of Management, Ahmedabad, one of the leading business schools in India, is summarised as follows (Ramachandran 1991).

1. The record of creating entrepreneurs is not too significant, especially considering the fact that the institute's primary thrust has been on creation of professional managers.
2. The institute has, of late, recognised entrepreneurship as an area that needs greater attention in teaching and research.

Countries like India, which belong to the second category, viz., learners, have come to catch up with leaders. A comparison by Patel (1997) after his visit to U.S.A. for collaboration and linkages with the leading business schools reveals the following:

1. In entrepreneurship competencies, intrapreneurship summer camps, micro enterprise development and comprehensive training programmes, India is ahead.
2. In family business growth programmes there is a lot in common.
3. In transfer of technology, commercialization of innovation, venture capital, global alliance we have a lot of catching up to do.

## Laggards in Entrepreneur Development

Countries like China are considered as the laggards in entrepreneur development. China began the process of entrepreneur development in 1978 after the introduction of Production Responsibility System. The surplus labour took entrepreneurship as the opportunity opened by the reform. As regard to education, a survey of microenterprises in Yunnan province of China, 6.7 per cent are illiterate and about 75 per cent had middle school education. There was not even a single person with college education. Those with higher education were reluctant to choose entrepreneurship. One of the reason is that the entrepreneurs enjoy lower social status (Wickramanayake and Wen Ming, 1996).

In a survey of graduate management students at three Chinese Universities, it became very clear that very few of the respondents wanted to do anything entrepreneurial. Most of them strongly aspired to become an official rather than to be owners of any business (Bennett, Lin and Litrack 1991). The management schools teach the management of government affairs and train them to become bureaucrats. A study by Van Auken and Changkee Su (1996) has observed that China is benefitted from the management experience and skills offered by Taiwanese entrepreneurs, for management of industries.

## Justification for Three Way Classification

To justify the classification of the countries around the world as leaders, learners and laggards—the continuum of entrepreneurial tendencies suggested by Burch (1986) can be used. The countries which can be considered leaders should operate in the extreme right of the continuum. That is, educating and training entrepreneurs such as innovative entrepreneurs and inventrepreneurs. USA is undoubtedly the leader in this area as per the comparison made by Patel mentioned earlier. Countries like India are on the threshold of stepping into the opportunistic entrepreneurs stage in the continuum. Looking at the laggards, the third category of the countries, China can be a good example because they are in the second stage of the continuum, viz., the bureaucrat. Thus, if we look at the classification of countries based on entrepreneurial tendencies, we can arrive at a conclusion that the whole world can be grouped under three—

leaders, learners and laggards. The leaders are active at one extreme, the laggards are at the opposite extreme and the learners are somewhere in between these two, may be in the middle of the continuum.

**Conclusion**

Culture plays a vital role in opting for entrepreneurial career. In countries classified as laggards, culture is a bottleneck for educated youth to get into business.

The entrepreneur development programmes are offered based on the local requirements and government policies. It starts with the initiative of industries development departments. As the education and training are important component of entrepreneur development, the task has been transferred to educational institutions. Mainly business schools have been transferred to educational institutions and have mainly contributed to the entrepreneur development. There are many different approaches to develop entrepreneurs. No one approach is universally accepted because each one has its own merits and demerits for a given situation. There are illiterate who are entrepreneurs, but formal and professional education and training help very much. The target group for entrepreneur development in most of the countries are those who could not get employment. In countries like USA the best students are opting for entrepreneurship career. There are also classification of entrepreneurship development activities such as for women, rural population, technocrats and the disadvantaged. NGOs are actively involved in helping the disadvantaged groups. Science and Technology Entrepreneurs Parks help technocrats. This means certain inputs are common to all groups and there are other things which are very specific to a gvien target group.

Entrepreneur development has taken the following route, awareness programmes—training—elective courses— graduate courses—post graduate degree courses—doctoral programmes —programmes for school students. Thus forward and backward integrations are taking place.

Major activities going on around the world can be grouped as:

1. Motivation
2. Support

3. Education
4. Skill development
5. Research

Entrepreneur development is relevant to single owner or micro enterprise or individual enterprise, subsequently managed as family business. In this context, small business management is also considered as part of entrepreneur development. Small business mean different ideas to different countries, because different criteria are used to define small business. The criteria used are investment, turnover and number of people employed.

Entrepreneur creates organisation and develops it. We can see a lot of activities directed at creating entrepreneurs. We need to understand an entrepreneur, before we develop one. Once we understand the entrepreneur, orienting our efforts to develop entrepreneur through education and training become simple. Until that time the experiment of developing entrepreneur will go on. There are certain things, institutions can offer and there are a few things which the entrepreneurs have to learn by themselves to become successful. Then the institutions operate with constraints which should be clearly pointed out to the students or trainees. Providing informational input and training alone cannot make a person a successful entrepreneur but the performance matters. The Entrepreneurial Development education and training activities going on around the world are not consolidated. Efforts are being made in this direction.

**Limitation and Scope for Further Research**

This Chapter has been prepared based on secondary data and interaction with experts working in the area of entrepreneur development. To collect complete details on the various entrepreneur development activities in the whole world, is not an easy task. Even ILO could not succeed in this because, it could collect data only from 26 countries of the world. Thus, there is a lot of scope for conducting further research to collect complete data from all the countries and make inferences. Such work will also enable the formulation of a comprehensive theory and practice in the area of entrepreneur development.

**References**

1. Bennet R., Lin J. and Litrack D. (1991), "Business values in the

Peoples' Republic of China: Barriers to Success,' *Proc.* 1991, ENDEC World Conference on Entrepreneurship Innovative Change, Singapore, Nanyang Technological University, pp. 54-58.

2. Burch J.G, (1986), *Entrepreneurship*, New York, John Wiley and Sons, pp. 30-33.
3. Dave R. (1997), 'Workshop on Entrepreneurship for Chief Co-ordinators of ED Cells', *Proc.* 1997, Ahmedabad, Entrepreneurship Development Institute of India, pp. 15-22.
4. INTERMAN (1991), 'Profile of Entrepreneurship Development Programmes—First Director', Switzerland, International Labour Office.
5. Katherine C. and Michael W. (1995), "The 25 Best-Business Schools for Entrepreneurs', *Success,* Vol. 42, No. 7, pp. 37-43.
6. Lord M. and Westfal G.R. (1996), 'Running Their Own Show,' *U.S. News and World Report*, pp. 88-89.
7. Meredith G.G. (1996), 'Entrepreneurs in Professional Doctorate Programmes', *Proc.* 1996, ENDEC World conference on Globalisation and Entrepreneurship, Singapore, Nayang Technological University, pp. 106-20.
8. Patel V.G. (1997), 'Entrepreneurship Education in USA and US', Entrepreneurship Development Institute of India, Reports No. 53, Ahmedabad, p. 1.
9. Prem S. (1995), 'Success of Entrepreneurship Development Programmes : An Evaluation Study', *Small Enterprises Development, Management and Extension Journal*, Vol. XXII, No. 2, pp. 1-9.
10. Ramachandran K. (1991), 'Entrepreneurship Education : Experiences of the Indian Institute of Management', *Proc.* 1991, National Workshop on Entrepreneurship Education in Management Schools—Agenda for Change, Ahmedabad, Entrepreneurship Development Institute of India, pp. 207-22.
11. Ray S. and Ramachandran K. (1996), 'Towards a Framework for a Comprehensive Theory of Entrepreneurship', *The Journal of Entrepreneurship*', Vol. 5, No. 1, pp. 1-22.
12. Scott D. (1995), 'Heretic in the Ivory Tower,' *Success*, Vol. 42, No. 7, p. 4.
13. TANSTIA (1991), 'Text of Small Scale Industrial Policy', Small Industry, Tamilnadu Small and Tiny Industries Association, pp. 23-29.
14. Van auken E.H. and Changkae Su (1996), 'A Risk Assessment of Taiwanese Investment in China', *The Journal of Entrepreneurship*, Vol. 15, No. 2, pp. 179-91.
15. Wickramanayake E. and Wen Ming (1986), 'Entrepreneurs in Micro-Industrial Enterprises in Yunnan Province of China', *Asian Entrepreneur*, Vol. 5:2 & 5:3, pp. 1-6.

# Index